BETWEEN HEAVEN AND EARTH

Richard Rowlands –
the life of an innocent man

Between Heaven and Earth

Richard Rowlands – the life of an innocent man

Nigel Thomas

Gwasg Carreg Gwalch

First published in 2023
© text: Nigel Thomas
© publication: Gwasg Carreg Gwalch

ISBN: 978-1-84524-535-1

Cover photo: Dorian Thomas
Cover design: Lynwen Jones

Published by Gwasg Carreg Gwalch,
12 Iard yr Orsaf, Llanrwst, Dyffryn Conwy, Cymru LL26 0EH.
Tel: 01492 642031
email: llyfrau@carreg-gwalch.cymru
website: www.carreg-gwalch.cymru

Printed and published in Wales

Dedicated to my wife Sally
for her help and patience.

With thanks to the following:
Dorian Thomas for support and help with the
graphics and photographs.
Mr Gerallt Jones for his help with structure and overall
encouragement.
The staff of the Anglesey Archives for their help and
patience.

Contents

Prologue

A few moments before eight o'clock on the morning of 4th April, 1862, Richard Rowlands, or Dic Rolant as he was called, husband, father, itinerant farm worker, bare fist fighter, seducer of women, and lately convicted murderer, stood on the hangman's drop. The scaffold had been erected on the east wall of Beaumaris gaol, and as the fatal hour drew near the large crowd that had gathered to witness the event, was whispering nervously.

The execution of the death penalty was being carried out upon the unfortunate man for the wilful murder of his father-in-law four months previously.

By the wretch's side, making the final preparations of his grisly trade was William Ong Calcraft, the official Home Office executioner, described as 'His Honour the Finisher of the Law' in the 1861 Census.

What thoughts ran through the head of Richard Rowlands at that moment? For certain the last thing on his mind was the church clock beside Steeple Lane, which he is said to have cursed, (he did not utter a word on the scaffold, having been persuaded not to do so by the ministers of religion who had attended him). He was more likely to be thinking of his soul, and of his myriad sins, for sins were more numerous in 1862.

Calcraft had checked everything. He favoured the 'short drop' allowing the condemned to fall three feet. This was sufficient to render him semi unconscious, but since the vertebra did not always break, death would often be by strangulation. Perhaps Calcraft considered it a just end, to suffer for causing suffering. A justification, perhaps an absolution for a man who was little more than a serial killer, albeit with the full blessing of the law. It was said that brandy salved what conscience he had left.

Punctual to the hour, the bolt was drawn and Richard Rowlands was no more, and Calcraft had earned his £18.

Said the balladeer, he was hanged 'Between Heaven and Earth'.

Chapter 1

The matter of the clock!

The Church of St Mary's and St Nicholas in the picturesque town of Beaumaris is quite imposing. Inside, although it has been subjected to restoration like many of our churches, its main impact is medieval. Heightening the effect is the impressive tomb of Sir Richard Bulkeley and his wife Elin, complete with their effigies, staring into eternity. Outside the church it is no less appealing with its weathered masonry and striking architectural features. It also sports a fine clock high on its tower.

The clock faces Steeple Lane, a narrow thoroughfare that is bounded on the western side by the gaol. The gaol, is in fact, the 'new gaol' and it was never an over-busy establishment, Anglesey being quite a law-abiding county. But its temporary gallows (erected especially for the executions) had dispatched two men. The first, William Griffiths for the attempted murder of his wife in 1830, and the second, Richard Rowlands was hanged in 1862 for the murder of his father-in-law.

William Griffiths' guilt is never questioned. The injuries he inflicted on his wife were horrendous and since attempted murder was a capital offence in 1830, he was sentenced to death. He died kicking and struggling, having first barricaded himself inside his cell by wedging his bed against the door.

Richard Rowlands, however, died quietly and bravely, and although the jury had unanimously found him guilty of wilful murder, after the execution of the death sentence upon him many began to doubt his guilt. This is because Rowlands continued to declare his innocence 'even under the most truth inducing circumstances'.[1]

The 'new' gaol in Beaumaris, replaced the old one on the green in 1829, and for its time it was considered a model example. The 1861 census (taken before Rowland's incarceration) showed a population of 11 inmates, there mostly for petty crimes and serving sentences of a number of weeks with hard labour.

The gaol is still there today and is open to the public, who can wander around its dark, oppressive interior and relive some of the fears of the inmates who were lodged there. The condemned cell is there, as is the door that led to the site of the temporary gallows. This was constructed as required in Steeple Lane facing the church and was accessed by a door set high in the wall that can be seen today. Also there is the old treadmill that formed part of the punishment routine. At least the treadmill served some purpose in as much that it pumped water into the gaol, the 'crank' on the other hand was a devise which served no real purpose at all. The prisoner had, for example, to turn it, say, 5000 times before retiring. It did nothing except keep count of the number of turns. People were sentenced to a custodial sentence for what we, today, would consider petty crimes.

Legend has it that he cursed the clock on the church

---

[1] *The Caernarvon and Denbigh Herald* which along with *The North Wales Chronicle* and *Yr Herald Cymraeg* are the main sources of primary evidence.

tower which he could have (only just) seen from the scaffold. He declared that that particular timepiece would never show the correct time, which, knowing the accuracy of church clocks, it probably never did! Whether Rowlands did indeed curse the clock at some time is uncertain. Every piece written about him in book or webpage, informs us that he did. If such a curse was uttered then it was done within the confines of the gaol for he spoke not a word from the scaffold, having been persuaded to adopt a course of silence by the ministers of religion attending him. He wished to declare his innocence, but they feared that he would be overcome by the emotion of the moment, and his fortitude might break down. They promised to publicise his declaration of innocence after his death. With this he seemed satisfied.

Many have found this man intriguing and there some who have written about him. Obviously, evidence would be scarce after such a long period of time, and no police records exist pertaining to the affair (all records prior to 1867 of the Anglesey Constabulary are missing, believed destroyed when the force at Holyhead moved into new premises). Apart from a few scraps here and there (the breakdown of the cost of his execution for example) the only direct evidence extant comes from the newspaper reports, mainly the *Caernarvon and Denbigh Herald*, *The North Wales Chronicle*, and *Yr Herald Cymraeg*.

Newspapers are notorious for their inaccuracies. Ideally their evidence should be checked against other sources, but in this case, there were none.

Thankfully, however, spurious as newspaper reporting was, with trials and inquests they tended to report statements verbatim, and since there were more than one newspaper interested in the affair then the accuracy of the report can be checked.

The story as it has come down to us has gathered a fair amount of extra baggage over the years, so care must be exercised. However, as the historian Philip Sugden says, myth attaches to the gaps in history and while an attempt must be made to separate fact from myth, both these aspects must be retained as both have their tale to tell. The tale of the clock tells us that at least in the popular imagination Richard Rowlands is innocent.

In order, however, to proceed some background information must be given the better to understand the period in question.

CHAPTER 2
A Very Rural Affair

Richard Rowlands, or Dic Rolant to give him his favoured name, and the main character in the story, was born in the parish of Llanrhyddlad quite close to the village of that name, and spent the last portion of his life (except for his time in prison awaiting trial and execution) in the adjoining parish of Llanfaethlu.

Both parishes account for a fair amount of land near the western coast of Anglesey. Even today they are very agricultural with farms joined by small, narrow roads. In the mid-19th Century this would have been more noticeable as the area was almost completely dependent on arable and pastoral farming. Small cash crops, a few cows, perhaps, provided most of the marketable produce, while a pig probably paid the bills or rent. Farms varied in size, but most were between 10 and 25 acres. Villages were self-sufficient in goods and services, but some change would almost certainly have been observed with the coming of the London Holyhead railway line in 1846. The railways were able to carry goods mass produced in the factories of England to the rural areas of Anglesey that could be sold at a price that would soon make the local artisan redundant. [2]

The exact area of interest to us is a relatively small one.

It consists mainly of four farms; Gaerwen, Tyddyn-y-Waen, Brynteg and Garnedd. Gaerwen was the largest at 101 acres and farmed by Owen Owen snr aged 43, and his son Owen Owen jnr aged 26 (this is how they were referred to in the newspaper reports). They were, as one might guess, father and son. Naturally their families lived with them. Tyddyn-y-Waen was 11 acres and farmed by John Jones at 48 years old, with whom lived his family. Then there was Brynteg of 22 acres farmed by William Jones aged 55, and his family. Finally there was Garnedd of 28 acres, farmed by Richard Williams aged 70, a widower who had just taken in his newly married (second time) daughter Elinor aged 35 and her 4 children by her first marriage ages ranging from 5 - 15. This assemblage of people is at the centre of our story.

It becomes quite clear by reading the evidence in the newspaper reports that this small group of farms must have formed an informal co-operative, where labour and scant resources were shared. "We helped each other in our farming" was a phrase used. For instance, expensive equipment, like the equivalent of today's combined harvester, would have to be hired, probably by the day, to complete certain tasks. In the 1860s it was the threshing machine that was called for. It would make more sense financially for all four adjoining farms to pool their resources and try to carry out these tasks at the same time. A threshing machine cost £20 to buy (a fair sum in those days) and some enterprising individuals would invest money in one and then hire it out to the smaller farms. Such was the case here.

---

[2] It is interesting to note here that it was the coming of the railways to Llannerch-y-medd (another Anglesey village that has lost a great deal of its original importance) that finally destroyed that village's boot and shoe-making industry. Factory made shoes were brought by the railway from Northampton and sold at a much cheaper price.

Three individuals owned the machine that made the rounds. Following the threshing machine from farm to farm was a group of itinerant workers that provided labour if it was required. Not being in permanent employment they were quite low down on the social scale and lived very much from hand to mouth.

As one would expect the people were deeply religious. There had been some questioning of belief during the 19th Century, a claim that is countered by many saying that this could not be true because of the number of revivals that occurred. It must be remembered, however, that for a revival to occur, there must first have been a decline, but it was a decline in people's faith in the clergy and to some extent organised religion. But belief in God in these rural areas remained quite sincere, and attending chapel (in the area under scrutiny, mainly the Methodist or the Baptist chapels) was still obligatory if one was to be judged 'respectful'.[3]

But while non-attendance at chapel or church was enough to brand a person a sinner, what offended most was overt sexual behaviour. Promiscuity in both the male and the female, self abuse, and even divorce were considered arch sins, but perhaps more than anything it was the conception of a child out of wedlock that most offended. Many women at the time who were unfortunate enough to have found themselves in this position committed suicide rather than face the social disgrace.[4] Even the newspapers shied away

---

[3] This continued until the 1950s where the numbers attending chapels were high. The situation deteriorated during the 1960s and has continued to do so. 4 See Dore's 'Drowned in the Thames' which depicts a young woman who has committed suicide by throwing herself in the river because she was expecting a child out of wedlock. So many people committed suicide in the Thames each year that, later, Tower Bridge, in whose nearby waters bodies seem to gravitate, has to this day its own mortuary.

from such a taboo subject, but anything else was fair game; murders, executions and accidents were reported in detail and often fathers would read every gory detail to their children as a moral lesson, hoping to keep them on the straight and narrow path. And, it must be remembered, newspapers were more widely read than before.

Wales was fortunate in that it had a very good system of Sunday Schools. This had developed over the years with pioneers like Gruffydd Jones, Llanddowror, campaigning for their establishment. What this meant was that a large number of the Welsh lower classes could read with some fluency. With the abolition of stamp duty on newspapers the price of an edition dropped to 1d (about half a new penny in today's money probably the equivalent of about 30p today) and thus became more affordable. The press was no less hungry for sensationalism and so would pounce on anything that they thought would increase their circulation.

It is worth noting here, also, the way people told the time. Today we are almost obsessed time, or rather with its accuracy. We have watches that are correct to about one or two seconds a month or even year. For most of the 20th Century the pips on the radio counted in the hour, and we are all familiar with the authoritative strikes of Big Ben heralding the hour. If asked the time, any one of us could probably as close to Greenwich Mean Time that any difference would be so small as not to matter. It was not always so.

In the mid-19th Century, there was no standard method of synchronizing time so it flew in every direction. Whereas in London it might be 12 midday, in Birmingham it could be quite different. There were even discrepancies over short distances. The time in any particular place was called 'Local Time'. And although it seems confusing today, it hadn't mattered then, for no-one needed such accuracy. The system seemed to work quite well in a time when people were ruled by the daylight hours and the calendar. Things were to change.

It was in the cities that the need for uniform time first became apparent. Businesses would need this accuracy when they dealt with other businesses. It even gave some enterprising individuals a living! On the top of Greenwich Observatory at precisely one o'clock in the afternoon, a red ball would descend a pole. There were some there who set a clock to this and then went around customers, businesses especially, selling the correct time. But outside of London the old 'Local Time' was still used. Then came something that accelerated the need for a universal time system.

That was the coming of the railways. It soon became clear that it was impossible to construct a workable train timetable without a uniform system of time. In the early years the problem was overcome by adopting the time at Greenwich, London, and carrying a chronometer on every train set to this time. At every station the clocks were synchronised to the train's chronometer, so ensuring that time was uniform throughout the rail network.

This time became known as 'Railway Time', but it did not supplant local time at first. The two systems would exist side by side for some time. There was the time that the trains arrived in and left the station and there was the time that people had always lived by. In Llanfaethlu, and probably other areas as well, however, there was an added complication, because there existed also 'Chapel Time', which was the time on the clock of the chapel. Despite this confusion the whole thing seemed to work.

Eventually, of course, the need for a uniform time system across the country was called for. In 1884 in the International

Meridian Conference in Washington DC, USA decided that the prime meridian should run through Greenwich rather than Paris, and it followed that the whole of Britain adopted Greenwich Mean Time as standard.

But the problem can be appreciated. Such a plethora of confused times reported in a trial where minutes were important. It was something that both police and law courts had to deal with. This brings us to the police.

Before the formation of organised police forces, peace was kept by parish officials known as constables. By 19th Century this system was under criticism generally because it was failing to deal with problems generated by a new urban society. The population was becoming more fluid, and crime, especially in towns was on the increase. The parish constables were usually old men, and it was fairly easy to get the better of them. Quite often they were on the receiving end of pranks. In 1829, Sir Robert Peel, the then Home Secretary, formed the Metropolitan Police in London, the first force of its kind, and after suffering immense unpopularity it had proved to be successful.

In 1856 the County and Boroughs Police Act made it compulsory for every county and borough to have its own force, and Anglesey responded in 1857 with the formation of the Anglesey Constabulary. Its birth was not without problems. A police force needed a Chief Constable, and the advertisement produced many candidates, twenty-three to be exact. It became obvious, however, that many of the candidates had been put forward by Justices of the Peace, to whom they were related. Sir Richard Bulkeley of Beaumaris, however, had other ideas. He was extremely influential, and one can see his mark on many projects on Anglesey at the time. He was determined that any holder of the office of Chief Constable should be Welsh speaking. With some perception he realised that the vast majority of the people of Anglesey were Welsh speakers, and so an English Chief Constable would be at a disadvantage. This narrowed the field considerably.

It was finally decided to offer the post to a Captain David White Griffiths who lived in retirement in Guernsey. He was a veteran of the Crimean War, who had served most of his time in the army in Malta. Having been a captain in the army it was thought that he would be able to 'handle men'. He had previously been the Lord Lieutenant of Caernarfonshire (I use the modern spelling of the town), and, more importantly, he was a fluent Welsh speaker. He continued in his post until 1876 when at the age of 60 he died suddenly. He was very much respected and a great many people attended his funeral in the cemetery of Llandysilio Church in Menai Bridge, where his simple grave can be seen today.

As Chief Constable he oversaw the establishment and early development of the Anglesey Constabulary. In reality Anglesey was a peaceful county. By 1861 the last murder had occurred 40 years previously, the murder of a young boy, and no-one had been brought to book for it. Much of the work of the new force was to do with the checking of weights and measures and keeping the peace, mainly in Holyhead, and especially around the docks. Notwithstanding all this the police generally were viewed with suspicion. They were considered to be something used by the upper classes to keep the lower classes down. Some considered them to be too expensive.

When the murder of Richard Williams occurred in 1861, it caught the attention of the press, which in turn stirred the public's emotions. It was the first serious crime that the force had ever had to deal with, and they *could not be seen to fail.*

Naturally there was no forensic science to aid them in a case where forensic science could have told them so much. Blood could be identified, but human blood could not be distinguished from the blood of, say, a sheep, or even a fish. There could be a bloody corpse and a bloodstained person standing within 10 yards of each other and there was no scientific method that could link the two. In fact even the Metropolitan Police did not have a forensic lab until 1934.

A police investigation often depended, therefore, upon an individual officer's knowledge of the local criminals, and in the absence of direct evidence, such as an eyewitness, they would try to establish who was last seen with the victim, who held a grudge against him or her, who profited from the death, was anyone acting suspiciously. In this way they would build a circumstantial case, in the hope that they could 'point a finger'. Before the case came before a court, however, three things had to be firmly established; means, motive and opportunity. This will be discussed later.

Chapter 3
Yr 'adyn' Richard Rowlands!

The word '*adyn*' in Welsh can mean different things. It can mean loner, wretch, or even outlaw. Whatever, as a description it is scarcely a compliment, and it was applied to Richard Rowlands.

His he was born on 19th November 1818 a son of Rowland and Sydna Williams of Tyddyn yr Eurych Llanrhyddlad Anglesey, and he was baptised in the Hên Bethel Calvinistic Methodist Chapel, Llanrhyddlad, Anglesey on the 20th December 1818. This would make him 43 in 1861, although most newspapers give his age as 45. He was one of 4 children (he had 3 brothers) born to the couple (Rowland died in 1855 and Sydna died in 1877 after being bedridden for some time). The family home in 1841 was Presaddfedd, and 'Rallt in subsequent censuses. These could possibly be the same dwellings having been renamed for some reason. The farm has now disappeared, so its position cannot be pinpointed with any degree of accuracy.

But it is not the only bit of confusion.

There is the question of why a man whose father was surnamed Williams was called Rowlands? This is rather difficult to explain, and the best would be conjecture.

There is no doubt that he was, according to the baptism

book, christened Richard Williams, but by 1842 (his first marriage) at least he was calling himself Richard Rowlands

This may have arisen because of the following.

Richard Rowlands was known locally as Dic Rolant. It could just be that he originally informally adopted the old Welsh mode of the surname, that being the Christian name of the father. So as his father's Christian name was Rowland, he would be Richard the son of Rowland, and rendered in Welsh as Dic Rolant. When asked officially for his name (census, marriage certificates etc.) he would have probably said 'Dic Rolant' which was translated literally into its English form, Richard Rowlands. This however is mere conjecture. So, what do we know for certain about him?

He first appeared in 1842 when he married one Emma Owens of Gwyddelyn farm, Llanbadrig, a fairly large parish in the north of Anglesey which contains the coastal resort of Cemaes. The marriage took place on 28th October 1842, in the old church of Llanrhyddlad (the present church is an entirely new structure). They went to live to Gwyddelyn where they had five children, John, Rowland, Hugh, Catherine and Jane. Little is known about his marriage other than the fact that it could not have been too successful. By 1851, according to the census of that year, Emma is living alone with her children in Gwyddelyn. She is designated 'head' of the family, and there is no sign of Richard. Neither is he to be found under his given name in the 1851 Census for Anglesey. A chance discovery in The Juror publication reported that a certain Richard Rowlands was involved in a skirmish in Caernarfon in 1851, where he was referred to as the 'despicable' Richard Rowlands. The census returns for Caernarfon show that there was a man by that name living there with a woman called Catherine. His age corresponds, but nothing else. It still remains a possibility that he is our man, since Richard was not the most honest of individuals. Some weight is given to this when we learn that when Rowlands was executed, his mother who was bedridden by then was told that he had gone [back] to Caernarfon. By 1853 Emma is dead, and the children have been put into the care of Richard's brother, who farmed Gamog in Llanrhyddlad.

There is no doubt that Richard Rowlands was considered the villain of the area, and it was said that he 'corrupted all who came in contact with him.' Whether this 'bad behaviour' was inherited is difficult to tell, for his brothers were respectable enough, but one commentator, Eigra Lewis Roberts, without giving a traceable reference (but is noted in several newspapers) believes that he took after his maternal grandfather who had the nickname 'Y Gwyddel' Owen Glyn, 'Gwyddel', the Welsh name for an Irish person. This could refer to a distant Irish ancestry or more likely it was probably used in a derogatory sense, as it meant someone 'wild and unruly' in the Anglesey dialect. So undisciplined was Richard Rowlands that he was refused membership of the Methodist Church when he applied for it during the religious revival of 1859. This rankled somewhat with Rowlands, because in a conversation with the minister in attendance when he was awaiting execution, he asked why he could not be judged for what he was now, as the sin he had committed was in the past. What this sin was is unclear, but in the condemned cell he admitted that his greatest sin was 'seduction'.

He appears again in April 1861, when the census captures a Richard Rowlands aged 40, born in Llanrhyddlad, residing in Gamog Bach, a farm near Llanfaethlu. His occupation was noted as being a 'farm labourer'. Although the age of this individual recorded does not tally with Rowlands' age of 43, there is little doubt that this is our man, and he comes into sharper focus after this point.

Sometime during that period of his life, or maybe a little earlier he either meets, or more likely, begins a relationship (for he almost certainly would have known of her) with one Elinor Roberts.

Elinor, as we have seen, was the daughter of one Richard Williams who farmed Garnedd in the Parish of Llanfaethlu. Elinor is first seen in the 1841 census as a girl of 15 living with her father (then a farm labourer) in nearby Llanfachraeth. (Richard Williams was a widower even in 1841, but his fortune improved because in 1851 he had acquired Garnedd, with 25 aces, and he was a farmer in his own right. By 1861 the size of the farm had increased to 28 acres).

Elinor married a stone mason from Holyhead called Robert Roberts and she had 4 children by him, Richard (15 years in 1861), Owen (12), Thomas (5) and Margaret (8). They lived in Holyhead and it was here that Elinor's bad luck began. Firstly, her husband died, and she and her children came to live with her father at Garnedd. She had a relationship with Richard Rowlands and was made pregnant by him some time around April, 1861. We know this with a fair degree of certainty because she delivered a child, a little girl, who was christened Anne at the end of December of that year. Since the confinement was said to be 'full term' April seems to be a likely date for conception. They were not married at the time, and this state of affairs must have rankled with Elinor's father Richard Williams.

Rowlands and Elinor were married in June of 1861 in the Register Office at Llangefni. Richard gave his age as 39 (he was infact 43), and so it appears on his marriage certificate. The reason that lay behind this is difficult to fathom, but it may be that people at this time genuinely did not know how old they were. It is also possible that he was just lying to impress a younger bride.

The marriage did a little to appease Richard Williams. He had forbidden Rowlands from coming to Garnedd, but he relented, probably after the marriage, and allowed him to visit occasionally. This was on condition that he and Elinor and the children should find alternative accommodation by All Saints (November 1st one of the Quarter Days when rents were paid and tenancies let). This he made plain to his neighbours during the corn harvest of 1861. This would be given attention during Rowlands' trial.

It may be that Elinor harboured a great deal of resentment against her father. The real cause may not be known, but it could possibly have been because of his decision to evict them. Evidence of this can be deduced from the newspaper reports of the Trial of Richard Rowlands in March 1862. A neighbour, William Jones of Brynteg Farm, had offered to arrange for a coffin to be made after Richard Williams had been found dead on the morning of November 2nd. He asked Elinor if the coffin should be of oak or of deal. Elinor answered that since it was deal that her father had intended 'for the children, then let it be deal.' Deal, of course, was the cheaper wood and sometimes pauper's coffins were made of it. The conclusion is that things were not well between Elinor and her father.

We know a bit more about Richard Rowlands. He was over 5 feet 10 inches tall, dark haired and with a dark beard. It was thought that he looked young for his age (one witness ventured 10 years younger), and that he was strongly built. One resident of Llanfaethlu said that he was remembered in the area as a 'hard' man who was well able to 'handle himself', and that he spent most of his time drinking in the Black Lion (a local public house), and that he frequently took part in bare-fist boxing matches.[5] This is local hearsay of course, but he had no regular job, and he 'followed the threshing machine from farm to farm'. It was also said of him that he was of above average intelligence, and that he had taught himself to read Welsh, although he could not write (he signed his marriage certificate to Emma with a cross). He was unable to speak English, as we shall discover later. In actual fact, for what it's worth, he seems to tick a number of boxes on the psychopathic profile. Superficially charming, habitual liar, manipulative, rationalising wrong doings, shallow emotions, ready to exploit the goodwill of others, sexually promiscuous, reckless behaviour, behavioural problems as a child, lacks inhibitions, no long term goals, short term relationships, no respect for authority, and finally intelligent. These traits are obvious in his character. Individually they mean nothing, but taken together they are significant. Time to move on.

---

[5] This part cannot be corroborated with hard and fast evidence, but it seems to be the general view of him in Llanfaethlu. Although it is anecdotal it is made of firmer stuff than the 'cursed clock', and it could even be true. It certainly fits in with what is known about him.

CHAPTER 4

'Have you heard anything about a house?'

Friday 1st November 1861, where the lives of a number of people were about to be turned upside down.

It was November. The time when the corn that had been harvested in the autumn was threshed. A new labour saving device had reached the little rural backwater. This was the threshing machine. Crude, certainly, when compared to modern day methods, but a thousand times better than the old way of threshing on the threshing floor with flails. The machine was probably powered by horses, and it would cut the time to a fraction of what it used to take.

This 'engine', as it was referred to (in Welsh probably *'peiriant'* or perhaps *'injan'*), would be hired by the day, and that a number of farms would share the cost of the hire. So it was that Elinor's two eldest boys, Richard and Owen, went to a farm called Tremoelgoch Bach, on November 1st, in the adjoining parish of Llanddeusant, to bring the engine to neighbouring Gaerwen Farm in preparation for the threshing on the morrow. They started at about 3 o'clock in the afternoon, and the journey there and back was going to take about 4 hours. It can only be assumed that Tremoelgoch had just completed its threshing and the 'engine' was moving on to its next place of employment, for Tremoelgoch did not own the machine. It is even possible that Rowlands had been working at Tremoelgoch during the threshing there, as that is how he earned his money. This is given added weight because he told a policeman after his arrest that he had been 'coming from Llanddeusant at about 6 o'clock.'

The boys arrived back at Garnedd, having first taken the 'engine' to Gaerwen at about 7 o'clock. Rowlands had arrived on one of his visits to the farm to see his wife at about seven o'clock, and had spent some time around the farm. It seems that the boys and he entered the farmhouse together.

Present in the house were Elinor, her two youngest children, and a lady called Ellen Hughes. They were now joined by Richard Roberts, his brother Owen and Rowlands.

Ellen Hughes needs some explaining. She was the niece of Richard Williams (farm owner) and had emigrated to America with her husband David Hughes. She was in the area visiting, and she had been at Garnedd since the previous Wednesday. This was the first time she had seen Richard Rowlands. She was always referred to as 'the American Lady' although it seems that she could speak Welsh fluently. Ellen Hughes was destined to play a major part in the proceedings that were to follow, but she does still remain something of a mystery.

The newspaper reports make it fairly easy to create a timeline for that night and all times were given in 'local time'. Richard Williams had set out for Gaerwen farm at about 6 o'clock to arrange for the threshing of his corn on the following day. To get there he had followed an old path across the fields that was not a public right of way, but just a 'path going from one place to another',[6] that the public used as a short cut. On the way he would have to negotiate a fence of about 4 feet high, set on an earthen bank, that

---

[6] Owen Owen Snr. *Trial CDH*

marked the boundary between the two farms. This did not worry him, because he had traversed it many times 'on his hands' (probably hands and knees) as one witness said.[7] The journey along this route to Gaerwen takes 12 minutes and it is a distance of just under 600 metres. So if he started off about 6 o'clock, it can be assumed that he would have reached his destination by 6:12, or 6:15 at the latest.

Almost as soon as Rowlands entered the farmhouse at about 7 o'clock his wife asked him if he had heard anything about a house. He answered vaguely that he 'might have'. If nothing else it shows that Elinor was worrying about a place to live, and emphasises the fact that Richard Williams really did intend to evict them if not that night then certainly the following morning. Owing to the way it is reported, one senses urgency in her tone. Almost immediately Rowlands asks, 'Where has the old man gone?' To which his wife answers that he had gone to Gaerwen.

It seems that he waited for just a short time in the house after this, but he could not have gone out immediately, as some commentators seem to imply. First of all, two of Elinor's sons were going to the 'Shoe Club' in the chapel, and needed money to pay their subscription. This was arranged before Rowlands went out.

'Shoe Club' needs some explanation, perhaps.

During the 1860s life was harder. There was a rigid class system that made social mobility difficult. Education was hard, although not impossible, to obtain, but it rarely allowed great movement between the classes. On top of that there were rigid morals, which governed the lives of the people especially the lower orders. Victorians valued sexual morality, Godliness, and cleanliness, and they also set store

---

[7] Owen Owen Jnr. *Trial CDH*

on thrift. They would proffer aid to those who were prepared to practice it. The Victorians were not as harsh as they are sometimes depicted, although it may seem so to us today. They were just different in as much that they could not abide poverty due to laziness but could sympathise with those who were poor through no fault of their own. They even divided the less fortunate into categories; the 'deserving poor' and the 'undeserving poor' where the former were given beneficial aid from the Parish, but the latter were consigned to the workhouse.

So 'clubs' were formed. There were Clothing Clubs, Penny Clubs, and Shoe Clubs, some of which continued well into the 20th Century. Although they were named differently, they pretty much amounted to the same thing. People, usually children, would attend a regular meeting, and bring with them a set sum every week, usually a few pence. This would then be handed to the overseer of the club, and it would be held for the donor. Over the weeks the sum built up until there was enough collected to buy either a pair of shoes, some clothing, or in the case of Penny Clubs, saved until a certain sum was reached. Financial advantages were gained through bulk purchases and donations from the richer members of the community who patronised the particular club. All to encourage thrift. Such was the club that Elinor's boys were going to attend on that evening.

In evidence Richard Roberts said that his 'mother gave me her money, and my father (Rowlands) gave me his money'. (It is interesting to note here that Richard Roberts calls his step father 'father').

It is only after this was seen through that Rowlands went out. He muttered something about having to go to 'some house' according to Ellen Hughes. This could have been a literal translation of a Welsh term, such as '*ty gwair*', translated means 'hay house' or it may have referred to an actual dwelling. The evidence does not reveal. However the important thing is that he went out a short time after, but not immediately after, he had entered Garnedd. This could have been as early as 7:15 local time.

What happens on the Garnedd side afterwards is not known, but it is possible to reconstruct what happened at Gaerwen.

Richard Williams stayed there for at least two hours, nearer two hours and a half. While he was there he chatted normally and smoked his pipe. He did not appear to be ill in any way, and to all appearances, although he was 70 years of age, he seemed perfectly healthy. Some time after 8.20 but possibly as late as 8:40 local time, he set off home the same way as he had come. The night was dark, and it was thundery weather. He seemed content enough though, and continued smoking his pipe. When asked if it was to dark for him, he said that it was 'right enough'. He was accompanied to the end of the farm buildings by Owen Owen Jnr. and he saw him walking steadily off across the fields. It is possible that he carried a lantern.

About seven minutes, later according to his evidence at the inquest, (the time it would take to reach the boundary fence) Owen Owen Jnr said heard a cry from the direction of the boundary fence which he thought had come from 'the men driving the horses into the field'. At the trial he said that he had heard a sound like quarrelling, and the voice of the 'old man shouting Richard'. He said that he recognised the 'old man's voice' but not the voice of the man quarrelling with him. This difference it will be appreciated is significant.

A man from Llynon Mill (probably the miller) was on his way home from Llanfairynghornwy about 9 o'clock that night, a road that would have given him a clear but distant view of the boundary fence in question, testified that the night was dark and thundery, but he was able to see clearly that there was a light there, probably from a lantern (see above). He thought that the light was stationary. He gives evidence at the inquest, but not at the trial which may be significant.

Richard Rowlands returned to Garnedd. Ellen Hughes said he returned between 1 hour and 1 ½ hours after he had gone out. This could mean anywhere between 8.15 and as late as 9 o'clock (this ambiguity was made much of by the defence at the trial). When he returned he washed his hands, something that he had not done when he had come in earlier that evening. He has a 'stirabout' by the fire (this was a kind of porridge made the Irish way by stirring hot water and oats together, rather than the Scottish way by which the oats were cooked. The mix was probably flavoured with salt). He had just mentioned that everyone was late returning to the house that night, when the boys returned from the shoe club. He went to bed about the same time as Ellen Hughes did, at 10 o'clock, pushing past her to get upstairs. The boys probably returned about 9:10 and were able to say that Rowlands 'was not out of the house any time while they were in'.

Richard Roberts and his mother Elinor stayed up waiting for Richard Williams to return, and they went to bed after 'supping the horses'. At no time did anyone go out to search for Richard Williams that night. In fact Richard Williams by all accounts did not like people fussing over him.

Chapter 5
'My grandfather is in a ditch ....'

By morning it was obvious that the old man had not returned home that night. It was given in evidence that he was often out late and on the occasions when someone went to search for him, he was, apparently, furious. Therefore they tended to leave him to his own devices. He had never, though, stayed out the whole night before. And there were other things that people noticed.

Ellen Hughes said that early in the morning she heard Richard Rowlands and Elinor, talking conspiratorially in a low tone, and sometimes whispering. Also, Richard Rowlands, contrary to his usual habit, seemed in no hurry to secure work with the threshing machine (it was probably employment on a 'first come first served' basis). The reason for this, he said, was that there was a fault with the wheel of the engine. It was not until seven that Richard Roberts Elinor's son was sent out to see if his grandfather had stayed at Gaerwen for the night. He only had to go as far the boundary fence to solve the mystery.

He came across the body of his grandfather lying near the boundary, on his left side with his head towards Garnedd and his feet in a ditch. He ran back and informed the household. 'My grandfather is in a ditch,' he said, and immediately Richard Rowlands and Elinor set off to the boundary fence. After a moment's thought they decided to ask William Jones of Brynteg to come along 'as he would know what to do'.

Evidence about the scene of the crime and injuries to the victim can be retrieved fairly accurately from evidence given at the inquest and trial.

Identifying the crime scene in the inquest, William Jones said that he accompanied Richard Rowlands to the scene and there was the deceased lying upon his side on the ground with his legs crossed. His legs were towards a ditch in a puddle of water. His head was lying in the direction of Garnedd and there was he maintained a great deal of blood near his head as there was also on the hedge over which the old man would have had to cross on his way home. He was talking about the boundary fence between the two farms. There was another fence, he said running from the boundary fence to Garnedd. At he end of this fence (the boundary fence end), he said, there was a gate with a pole across the gap

In the evidence William Jones gave at the trial he more or less confirms this, but much of what else he said goes to implicate Rowlands. This will be dealt with in its appropriate place.

Further information can be gathered from the depositions of Richard Williams' son, William Williams of Trefdraeth (a small community on Anglesey some miles from Llanfaethlu), who came to Garnedd on Monday 4th November.

Richard Rowlands, he said, came to show him the place where the deceased was found. Williams asked him about the blood on the top of the wall. Rowlands replied that it must have been done by Richard Williams falling there on his nose. Williams did not believe that so much blood could result from nose bleed, but Rowlands could find nothing to say in response to that, and they both left the scene together.'[8]

Inspector Richard Ellis of Holyhead Police Station gives us some more information about the crime scene.

He examined the spot where the body was found. Sergeant Parry and Constable Robert Griffith both of Holyhead Police Station had pointed out the place to him. He found at the top of the fence between Garnedd and Gaerwen considerable blood. Mostly on the side next to Garnedd. In a primitive attempt at forensic science possibly he cut out the sod from off the fence. Within four inches to that spot he observed a hole in the fence which might have been made by a pickaxe or the point of a hammer. Apparently the ground had been a little trampled. He also mentioned a cross fence running from the boundary up to Garnedd in a N.W. direction, and that the body was said to him to be found on the field side as you come from Gaerwen to Garnedd. There was some blood on the stones and also on the ground, he observed and he measured the distance from the top of the fence where the blood was first found and that on the field. It was eleven feet exactly. The distance from the boundary fence to Garnedd is about 219 yards. This is a fairly accurate measurement.

Mr Edward Williams of Llanfachraeth was the surgeon who performed the post mortem examination on Richard Williams. It gives a full account of the injuries, internal as well as external that the victim suffered. It is worth recording this verbatim.

'I was at Garnedd on Monday. I examined the body of the

---

[8] William Williams. *Inquest CHD NWCH YHG*

deceased. I cut off his hair. The first wound I examined was a little above the right ear. It was about an inch and a half in length. It had not penetrated the bone. But below there was a depression of the temple bone. On the vertex of the head there were two longitudinal wounds the one next to the right ear was two and a half inches long the other about two inches. They were both scalp wounds without any fracture. On the upper point of the left ear was a slight lacerated wound above which was a slight aberration, and about two inches and a half in the posterior there was another scalp wound one and a half inches in length. On Tuesday last I made a post-mortem examination along with Dr Price of Holyhead. We examined the head and body. Upon removing the scalp there was considerable extravasations from ear to ear. The right side of the temporal lobe was shattered and completely battered in injuring the dura mater to a depth of an inch. There was also a transfer fracture of the scull from the right temporal bone to the left side. Also above the right ear there was a fracture extending to the back of the scull. The rest of the body was healthy. In my opinion the wounds could not have all been inflicted with a sharp instrument. They must have been inflicted by the sharp as well as the blunt point of instruments such as the hammer produced. I have no doubt that those wounds caused the death of the deceased.' [9]

His evidence was corroborated by Mr J R Price, Surgeon of Holyhead. The evidence given at the trial by the surgeon is the same as that given at the inquest.

From these sets of evidence a number of things can be learned.

Firstly, the scene of crime can be quite clearly pinpointed;

_____

[9] Edward Williams, Surgeon *Inquest CDH NWCH YHG*

no other interpretation makes sense when the attitude and position of the corpse are taken into consideration. Secondly, it would appear that the attack on Richard Williams occurred on the top of the boundary fence, and that he fell from there into the field, hence the blood on the top of the fence and on the field. It is possible that he was alive for some time while lying in the field, because it is obvious that his blood was still flowing, and blood will not flow after the heart stops. Thirdly, the injuries to the head were extensive, suggesting a frenzied attack. Such attacks are usually perpetrated by someone who knows the victim. Fourthly, the injuries sustained would be classified as blunt trauma today, that is, blows by a blunt instrument. Finally the primitive state of police methods, especially forensic science methods, becomes obvious.

Chapter 6
Digging a Deep Hole

When we think of crime scenes today, we see people in white coveralls, gloves and white disposable boots, handling expensive equipment, photographing, measuring, and taking notes. The crime scene is isolated and preserved; evidence has to be carefully handled; each separate item must be bagged, labelled and signed for when it changes hands. Only in this way can the integrity of that particular piece of evidence be maintained. There must be no hint of contamination. In these days of DNA testing the verdict of a court may hang on a follicle of a hair, or a stain smaller than the head of a pin. In 1861 such things were in the future, but it still surprises us that as many as eight people contaminated that crime scene, and not only that, they went for a cart, and took the body away from the scene immediately. However such was the way that things were done.[10] The first duty of the police on finding a dead body was to certify the absence of life and to remove the body as quickly as possible.

---

[10] Even in 1888 during the Ripper scare in Whitechapel and Spitalfields, it was the duty of the police to remove the body as quickly as possible, which explains why, perhaps, that even though photography was available, no crime scene photographs were taken except in the case of Mary Kelly (photographs of the other victims were taken in the mortuary).

After the body of the deceased was taken home we know that Richard Rowlands went to Trefdraeth (somewhat to the south-east of Llanfaethlu) on the dead man's mare. It would appear that Richard Roberts Elinor's son accompanied him, and he gives a starting time of 10 o'clock. In Ty'n Llwyn, Trefdraeth lived the aforementioned William Williams, Richard Williams' son. The journey would have taken about 4 to 5 hours, and he arrives between two and three o'clock in the afternoon. Williams had never seen him before, but knew of him. Rowlands informs him that his father has died, and Williams was anxious to know how it happened. Rowlands explained that he had gone to 'Gaerwen or somewhere' the previous night and that he had gone over a hedge where timber had been put to prevent the cattle from escaping, and that he must have fallen, and that the fall had induced a fit. Rowlands said he felt it was the darkness of the night that was to blame. Williams wanted to know why his sister Elinor had not gone to search for him to which Rowlands answered that that was a failure on their part.

Rowlands wanted William Williams to come to Garnedd with him immediately, but he refused, saying (rather strangely perhaps, considering that his father was dead) that he would go there on Monday. 'Come early, before the inquest,' implored Rowlands, 'before people have time to speak'. A sure sign that he was aware that tongues would wag. Williams did go to Garnedd on the Monday and visited the crime scene. He noticed the blood on the wall, and commented upon it. Rowlands maintained that that was where he 'fell on his nose', to which Williams replied that no-one bled from his nose in that way, and that the 'hedge was full of it'.

It seems certain from the tone of the evidence that William Williams had severed all ties with his sister probably because of her marriage to Rowlands. Rowlands he had not met, but the impression is gained that he did not approve of him, neither was he at his wedding to his sister. He also exhibits a certain callousness when he refuses to go to Garnedd on the Saturday be with the family.

Of the Saturday night of the 2nd November we have no information, but Sunday was to bring another facet of the case into focus, thanks to Richard Roberts the grandson and Ellen Hughes, the so called 'American woman'.

By Sunday the 3rd of November the news had spread like wildfire around the district, and so had the gossip and rumour.

At the inquest Ellen Hughes remembered:

'On Sunday morning Richard Rowlands desired me not to say anything that he had been out of the house after he returned on Friday night.' [11]

Later at the trial she said:

"On the Sunday all the family and myself were in the same house. He said we will sit down by the fire to speak of what we shall say when called upon. He wanted us to persist in saying that he had not been out of the house and if they did so no one could do anything to him. Before he said that he said that the servant of Bronheulog had said that he had killed the old man. I do not recollect that well. The following day the daughter and I went to Llanfachraeth. He desired his wife to prevent us from going and asked, would no other day do as they might testify at Garnedd that he had not been out of the house that night after he first came in."

It was mentioned by Richard Roberts in the trial that Rowlands had learned that the servants of Bronheulog and 'Rallt were talking about him and saying that he had killed

[11] *CDH NWCH YHG*

the old man. Rowlands promised to 'law' [12] the servants after the inquest.

Richard Roberts also deposed that on the Sunday night, Rowlands had brought all the family together. He said in evidence:

'I recollect the Sunday night[13] sitting around the fire he (Rowlands) wished to advise us all to say the same thing. That it was likely we should be examined, and we were to mind not to say that he had been out.'

Ellen Hughes has no axe to grind. She was not of the area and she would have no motive to lie. Furthermore she appears to be a fairly simple minded person, who could be confused (something the defending counsel at the trial made use of), but on this point as well as on the point that Rowlands went out a second time she did not waver even under rigorous cross-examination. It was also asking much of these people to lie to the police and later commit perjury in a court of law. It was rather presumptuous for Rowlands to expect this from Ellen Hughes having never met her before this weekend, but it may hint at his own disregard for the truth, and also to his desperation. But although Rowlands' behaviour was regarded as suspicious, it is clear that he was aware that he was under suspicion, and he was genuinely asking for the family's help, because he had no alibi for the critical time. It is evident however that Ellen Hughes did not make her refusal clear at the time, because even after his arrest and his incarceration in the police station at Holyhead he was still maintaining that the *American Woman would say that he had not gone out a second*

---

[12] Probably meaning 'sue'.

[13] The subject seemed to have been discussed in the morning and in the evening, and it was obviously praying on Rowlands' mind.

time' on the night of 1st of November. And so Sunday became Monday, and at Holyhead Police Station the machinery of the police was finally rumbling into action.

Chapter 7
The Police Investigate

Almost three days had elapsed and no police had visited the scene. But to be fair, this was the way things were done in those days. Forensic science was all but unheard of and police methods, as already explained, were totally different.

The job of investigating the death of Richard Williams fell to Inspector Richard Ellis of Holyhead Police Station. Ellis was one of two inspectors (the other was at Menai Bridge Police Station) that had been appointed to the new Anglesey Constabulary. He was possibly the Richard Ellis who had served as constable in Amlwch parish before the formation of the new force. Holyhead police station was housed in 19 Newry Street Holyhead, and would remain there until 1867. It had all the usual lock-up facilities, but so far these had only been used to incarcerate drunks and brawlers. Richard Ellis was married and had two children. His family lived with him at the station.

Inspector Ellis heard of the Garnedd incident on the Sunday night of the 3rd November, when he was told by Sergeant Griffiths of the death of Richard Williams. It would appear that he reached there about mid-day. He went to the crime scene and described it in enough detail as we have seen to enable recognition. He searched the farm and found a hammer in the cow-shed that he thought could have been the murder weapon. He sought out Richard Rowlands and confiscated some of his clothing; a jacket; a pair of trousers and two shirts one of which Rowlands was wearing (he was actually wearing two) and he had to take it off. It was not known if Ellis was at this time aware that Ellen Hughes and Margaret Roberts were able to testify that he had been out a second time that night and could not account for his whereabouts satisfactorily. At least Rowlands was not aware of any such interview because he still maintained later that he had not been out and that the 'American woman' would say the same. Whatever the case, Rowlands was arrested, and Ellis must have been satisfied that he had a motive in that he and his pregnant wife were supposed to be evicted from the farm on the very night that Richard Williams died; means in the hammer he found; opportunity in as much that Rowlands had no real alibi for the time of the murder.[14]

He was taken to the lock-up in Holyhead Police station and he was attended by Constable Michael Toohill who heard him say to the Inspector Ellis that '*Whatever killed the old man, that hammer never did.*' This was later used in evidence against him, strangely, because if it was not the hammer that killed Richard Williams then means had not been proved. The evidence is slightly contentious as some maintain that it was strange for him to make any comment about a hammer when he supposedly did not know of its existence. It is not impossible however that Ellis had mentioned it to him when he was being questioned. Constable Robert Hughes deposed at the trial that Rowlands had told him that he had come home to Garnedd and joined the boys in the stable. He stayed there until half past seven

---

[14] Today all this would seem to be rather a weak case.

then went to the house went to bed by 10 after having coffee for supper (this was untrue as Ellen Hughes deposed later that he had the aforementioned 'stirabout') and that he had not gone out a second time that fateful night and that the American woman would testify to this. Bizarrely he then asked Constable Hughes to pray for him saying that it *'was hard in this life but how would it be in eternity.'*

On the Tuesday it would appear that Ellis dragged the pond, presumably to try to find a murder weapon, but with no result. Again the question of means is doubtful.

Much of the above information comes from what the newspapers report about the inquest held into the death of Richard Williams. A more detailed scrutiny of the proceedings tells us a little more.

CHAPTER 8
Inquest into the death of Richard Williams

The Coroner is obliged to hold an inquest if a death is suspicious or if the cause of death is unclear. This makes the Coroner's Court one of the most powerful in the land as he needs no higher power to authorise its convention. Its job however is to determine the time and cause of death, and to record anything pertaining to the matter incase such evidence is needed in the future if the case is reinvestigated. The coroner for Anglesey at this time was Mr William Jones. He had gained the post after a closely fought contest, and was to remain as coroner for 40 years.

The inquest into the death of Richard Williams opened at about 2 o'clock on Monday 4th November 1861, at the Black Lion public house near Llanfaethlu which still stands today.

It was not uncommon to hold inquests in such places as they were able to offer all facilities including refreshments. It was adjourned, however, after hearing only part of the evidence of William Jones of Brynteg, and the adjournment coincided with the arrest of Richard Rowlands. A post mortem examination was ordered on the body of Richard Williams, after which the court reconvened on Thursday 7th November, this time in the Baptist Chapel. Richard

Rowlands was present and he was represented by Mr R D Williams a solicitor from Caernarfon. Also present was the Rev. James Williams of Llanfairynghornwy, a Justice of the Peace, and the Chief Constable of the Anglesey force, Captain David White Griffiths.

The whole thrust of the questioning appears to be to implicate Richard Rowlands, which was really beyond its mandate. Questions about Rowland's relationship with the deceased abound, and when Ellen Hughes gives evidence that he went out from Garnedd on the night of the murder and stayed out for about one to one and a half hours, and that he had asked her to provide him with an alibi (basically asking her to perjure herself) people were beginning to make up their minds.

Apart from the fact that the inquest provides much of the information that is known about the case a few other things are worthy of note.

Firstly, viewed today, the evidence given, apart from that of Ellen Hughes, and pointed questions notwithstanding, is not totally damning to Rowlands. Even Ellen Hughes' testimony can hardly be called entirely impartial. What is notable is the lack of direct evidence. The police were aware of this and attempted to introduce some, albeit clumsily. When giving evidence Inspector Richard Ellis would say that he had examined the clothes he had taken from Rowlands as evidence and found a mark on a pair of trousers that in his opinion was blood. This was too much even for the rather biased coroner and he mildly rebuked the Inspector for speculating.

Secondly, some things were given in evidence that would later be exaggerated and even changed or added to in the trial. More of this later.

Thirdly there were witnesses in the inquest who gave

evidence that could have been used at the trial, but was not. A man walking from Llanfairynghornwy to Llynon Mill said that at nine o'clock he saw a light, probably a lantern, at where the crime scene would have been. The time of nine o'clock would be uncomfortably close to the time when Richard Rowlands was known to be back in Garnedd.

Fourthly, the police being painfully aware of the dearth of evidence were beginning to set things up. Inspector Ellis deposed that he had heard Richard Rowlands say that he didn't think *'that there was any enmity between the old man (Richard Williams) and anybody except William Jones.'* At this point William Jones must have sat up in indignation and with a little apprehension perhaps. He had already given evidence and his testimony was neutral towards Rowlands. This was a cunning ploy on the part of the police, and probably not altogether honest as Richard Rowlands, even near to his execution, said that the police had worked up a case against him, and had *'told lies'*. It is significant that later in the trial it is the evidence of William Jones and his alone that provides the missing link between Rowlands and the crime scene, and proves to be a huge nail in his coffin.

In his summing up the coroner said in a case that he 'did not hesitate to say was the result of a deliberate act of cold-blooded murder, it was important that their minds should be free from all idle rumours that were flying about as usual in such cases ... there is little doubt that poor man Richard Williams had been murdered, but the question was by who?'. After having urged impartiality on the jury he then set about to destroy it.

He thought that it was impossible to bring the guilt home to anyone but the prisoner Rowlands. He gave his reasons. 'There was no one else', he opined, 'in the house that had full knowledge of knowing where when and which way the old man was likely to return that could have done it but the prisoner'. Also, 'Why could he have not come forward to tell the whole truth about his absence from the house on the occasions sworn to by some of the witnesses ... why did he call for water to wash his hands on his second appearance at the house more than the first when he had just returned from his work.' They had it 'that he was out for about an hour and a half and what he did then [only] God Almighty knew.'

He asked them to examine his subsequent conduct.

At this point Captain David White Griffiths reminded the Coroner of the evidence of Ellen Hughes and the remark made to her on Sunday by the prisoner, i.e. that he had asked them in the house not to let anyone know that he had been out of the house a second time on Friday evening.

The jury naturally brought in a verdict of 'wilful murder by Richard Rowlands.' It should be noted here that up to 1977 an inquest jury could actually name a suspect in its verdict.

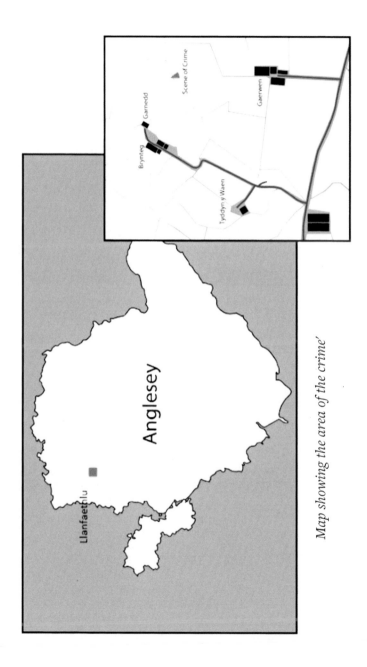

Map showing the area of the crime'

51

Rowlands Grave Site *Judge Henry Keating*

Garnedd

David White Griffiths

David White Griffith's Grave

Door to Scaffold

Door onto the scaffold in Steeple Lane

William Calcraft

Henry Harris Davies -Pererin   *Morgan Lloyd*

Crime Scene Today

Black Lion

CHAPTER 9
Hiatus

The case had attracted a great deal of interest mainly on account of its novelty and the press' newly found popularity. One would have expected long lasting episodes of correspondence in the much used letter columns of the *Caernarvon and Denbigh Herald* and *The North Wales Chronicle*, as well as *Yr Herald Cymraeg*, but as it happened this did not materialise. It was to do so later, but now something else claimed the press' attention.

On the 23rd of December 1861, Albert, the Prince Consort, and much beloved husband of Queen Victoria died and the press were deluged in grief. This put paid to any speculation about Richard Rowlands (now languishing in Beaumaris gaol) and the Llanfaethlu murder. All we know about him at his time is that he was quiet, gave no trouble, and that he did not let his predicament interfere with his appetite.

And so the year died and the New Year was ushered in with still more grieving for Prince Albert. We know nothing further of Rowlands until his trial on the 22nd March 1862, which was a Saturday.

CHAPTER 10
Pointing a finger

Rowlands had been imprisoned awaiting his trial since the 4th of November 1861 when he was arrested. He had first been incarcerated in the lockup in Holyhead Police Station and taken to Beaumaris on the 7th. The trial was to take place at Beaumaris Courtroom opposite the castle. This building has been a court since the 17th Century and has been opened in modern days as a museum. It has seen many an interesting trial. Apart from Richard Rowlands, there have been William Griffith, and later early in the 20th Century William Murphy and Sion 'Lias who have received capital sentences there. (Murphy was hanged in Caernarfon Gaol but Sion 'Lias was later reprieved). Even today some of the grimness of its function remains in its stark decor.

Presiding was Sir Henry Singer Keating a prominent judge on the North Wales Circuit, who later rose to become Master of the Pleas.

Defending was Morgan Lloyd a barrister originally from Trawsfynydd, and later a Member of Parliament. Prosecuting was Mr McIntire (Christian name not known) and Mr Trevor Parker. McIntire and Lloyd had more or less carved up the work on the Circuit between them and this was not the first time they had faced each other.

The jury consisted mainly of the local gentry.

Here it must be appreciated that it is the job of the police to find the perpetrator of a crime, the jury is charged solely with the task of deciding whether the person in the dock is in fact the perpetrator. The jury must also be satisfied beyond a reasonable doubt that the defendant is guilty or they must find in his or her favour.

The following is a list of the jurors who heard the case:

W B Hughes Plas Coch (Foreman)
J Williams Treffos
J L Hampton Lewis Henllys
Major-General R Hughes Bryndu
H Pritchard Trescawen
H O Williams Trecastell
W B Panton Holyhead
W Massey Corris
R J Hughes Plasllwyncoed
H Webster Ty'n Pwll
R W Jones Beaumaris
R E Owen Hendref
E O Pierce Llanfaes
W Walthew Holyhead
W Parry Lewis Cichle
J W Paynter Maesllwyd
W J Holt Plas Cadnant
Stephen Roose Syr Rhys
P B Edwards Beaumaris
T Lewis Hampton (T Hampton Lewis?) Henllys
Ll Jones Beaumaris

The list contains a number of prominent names that can be found on any book about the history of Anglesey in the late 19th and early 20th Centuries. They were certainly not of the same social class as Rowlands.

It is unfortunate that the two people whose evidence would have been most interesting were not allowed to testify, namely Rowlands himself and his wife Elinor. This was because at the time the defendant was not allowed to take the stand in case he was tempted to lie in the emotion of the moment and thus 'imperil his immortal soul', and even today spouses cannot give evidence against a partner.

Interest in the case had rekindled and the press proclaimed that important new evidence was to be adduced. People flocked to the courtroom and such was the clamour that the judge ordered that the room be cleared if order was not kept. As it was women and children were prohibited from entering, an action that was praised by the press because after the initial skirmish good order was preserved throughout the proceedings. Sir Henry was conscious of the fact the case that was to come before him was a serious one and that in a county well known for its law abiding ways.

The trial opened in the usual way with the prosecutor Mr McIntire making the opening statement, and set out the case against Rowlands. In British law the defendant is given the presumption of innocence until he or she is proven guilty. This means that it is not the work of the defence to prove the innocence of the prisoner. A defence attorney need not necessarily have to believe in the innocence of his client (although it helps if that belief is present). His or her job is to point out weaknesses in the prosecution's case.

McIntire began by stating the charge against Rowlands which was the wilful murder of Richard Williams on the 1st November 1861. He then summarises the circumstances of the crime before stating what he intended to prove against the prisoner. As was usual he warned the jury that 'the case must be proven clearly to their minds and if they entertained doubt then they must give the prisoner the benefit of that doubt.'

McIntire pointed out that Rowlands and his wife were to leave the farm on that day which was considered to be 'motive' enough for the murder. Also when Rowlands returned from work that night he enquired about the old man and when told where he was he went out immediately and did not return until between 8 and 9 o'clock. This said McIntire showed that: '*at the time the old man met his death the prisoner had left the house and was in the immediate neighbourhood* and 'opportunity' was considered established. The fact that he called for water to wash his hands after he had been out a second time that night was also considered suspicious. Rowlands explanation that he had dirtied his hands trying to mend the engine[15] (it had apparently a broken wheel) although entirely plausible carried no weight.

Witnesses were called and are treated here in order of importance rather than the order in which they appeared at the trial.

The next part of the case could perhaps be considered contentious. William Jones' evidence at the inquest was bland and non-accusatory. Now however the whole tone of his testimony changes. Rowlands came to him on the morning of Saturday 2nd, he said. He immediately observed some 'blood on his whisker' He went on,

'I saw it exactly like blood. He wiped the clean side of his face and I told him that is not the side, it is the other side. He turned after he wiped it, and asked, is it clean now. I said

---

[15] Ellen Hughes. *Trial CDH NWCH*

no, it is there still, and there I saw it the last thing after I spoke to him.' [16]

Rowlands also continued to try to persuade Jones that the old man had met with some accident and that he had not been murdered *'for what had he for any person to get?'* Next Jones noticed a footmark. This part of the evidence is reproduced here in full as it was an important part of the prosecution's case.

'I saw the prisoner walking backwards and forwards. I called to him saying that the body had been dragged, and we aught to see if there were any footmarks. I cannot see any other footmark but this, a narrow footmark with small marks on it. The prisoner said that is my footmark this morning. I said it appears to me that it was made last night. I said so because there appears to be water in the nail marks: it had rained during the night. The mark was near a (sic) body. After raising the body to the cart, I saw a corresponding footmark, only one was the right and the other was the left. I pointed with my finger and said to the prisoner, that is a mark of a foot since last night, or since the body was placed there. The prisoner put his foot upon it. I said fair play, some persons will come here tomorrow to examine the footmarks.' [17]

Jones contended that the inquest would not pass without saying that Richard Williams had been killed. Whereupon Rowlands responded by saying that if Jones was at the inquest he was to be careful not to say that Richard Williams had been killed, a plea he reiterated when he took leave of Jones later. On complaining of being cold Rowlands said that he was wet last night. Jones was shocked he said and asked

---

[16] William Jones' testimony at the trial as reported in the CDH and NWC

[17] William Jones testimony at the trial as reported in the CDH and NWC

if Rowlands had been out last night to which Rowlands answered no. Jones reflected that it was lucky that the 'American woman' was there, for she is the person who will save you. Jones concluded his evidence by asserting that there had never been a cross word between Richard Williams and himself, and that in fact they used to assist each other with their farming. The seed Inspector Ellis had sown in the inquest had obviously germinated.

It becomes apparent that Jones' deposition is more damning at the trial to what it was at the inquest. Morgan Lloyd picked this up, to which William Jones answered that he was frightened at the inquest but he had divulged it to certain officials. Another thing that is worthy of note is the fact that, if the testimony is correct, Rowlands is becoming scared.

Ellen Hughes, the so-called American woman, had not acceded to Rowlands request to lie for him and give him an alibi. Her evidence was much as it was in the inquest except that now she stated quite definitely that he was out of the house for one and a half hours, not the one hour that she had adduced then.[18] The judge commented on the fact saying that the witness' evidence was 'more favourable' than that which she had given at the inquest.

Margaret Roberts, Rowlands' step daughter, confirmed Ellen Hughes statement, but said rather ambiguously that it was 'past eight when he returned' which given the haphazard time systems could mean any time after eight o'clock!

McIntire made the point that no blood was found on Rowlands' clothes, indeed a Dr Taylor had examined them,

---

[18] It is worth noting perhaps that it was Ellen Hughes alone among the witnesses, apart from the officials who was able to speak English, and therefore fully understand the proceedings.

and he could not find a trace of blood on them. He also made the point that a hammer was found and exhibited at the inquest and it was assumed that this was the murder weapon. Inspector Ellis and Constable Michael Toohill both said that they had heard Rowlands say while in custody in Holyhead Police Station that whatever killed the old man 'that hammer never did', suggesting to them, probably, that Rowlands knew what the real murder weapon was.

The testimony of Owen Owen Junior is also contentious. It will be remembered that at the inquest he said that he had heard a cry from the direction of the boundary fence about seven minutes after Richard Williams had departed on the fateful night, a cry that at the time he attributed to the men who were driving the horses into the field it was that vague. That he was able to state with some conviction that the cry occurred after 'seven minutes' speaks well for his assessment of the passage of time when all other witnesses were ambiguous in their assessments. Now when he took the stand, he said that it was a sound of quarrelling that he had heard and the sound of the old man's voice shouting 'Richard'. He admitted that he recognised the voice of Williams but not the other voice. He also said when questioned that he had known Rowlands all his life. It is difficult not to believe that some coercion had happened.

Thus was the case against Rowlands. Now it must be remembered that this was the mid 19th Century and in the absence of direct evidence such as an eyewitness, all the prosecution could do was to gather circumstantial evidence until there was enough to 'point a finger', so we must not cavil too much at the police, but it cannot be stressed enough.

The prosecution's case, therefore, shows that although opportunity was proven, the motive offered appears to be weak. The weapon that was used had not been satisfactorily accounted for, but this could be given as a blunt instrument, and Rowlands had access to plenty of those on the farm. More importantly, perhaps is the failure to pinpoint the exact time of death, which appears to have been placed in a time bracket of about half an hour. Although there is no evidence for it, one must assume that there had been a formal identification of the body, said by some police officers to be the cornerstone of any investigation.

The prosecution had managed to place the prisoner at the scene of crime through the witness William Jones and less convincingly, probably, through the witness Owen Owen Junior, strengthening the 'opportunity' part of the charge. The blood on the whisker, the footprints or footmarks as they were referred to, and the virtual admission by Rowlands to Jones that he had been out the previous night in the rain all spoke against the accused. Whether this was strong enough to convict in a trial for a capital offence is another question, and it is open to debate. Also, it must be remembered that most of the damning evidence was in the testimony of one witness.

So having heard this, what did the defence make of it?

Chapter 11
The life of an innocent man

Now the reader will remember that it is the work of the defence team to point out flaws in the prosecution's case. The question is; did Lloyd do this properly? It is difficult to know how much the press had summarised the address, but Morgan Lloyd's presentation takes mere five minutes to read.

He started by warning the jury that this was a serious case and, reiterating the words of the Coroner in the inquest, that they must free their minds of idle rumour. In other words the prisoner was to be tried for the crime with which he was charged, and not for something they believed he had done in the past, nor must they give any credence to rumours they may have heard. They were to try the case on the evidence alone. *'Do not,'* he pleads, *'come to a hasty conclusion as there was the life of a man in their hands.'* This hints at the fact that Rowlands had transgressed in the past.

He refers to the prosecution's 'principal point' that Rowlands had gone out after the old man and was therefore in the vicinity when the crime was committed. This proved very little, he said, as there were many other people out at the same time as well (this we have from Owen Owen Junior at the inquest when he said that he heard a cry from the direction of the boundary fence and thought it was from the men driving the horses into the field, also from Richard Roberts who said that he and his mother Elinor 'supped' the horses at 9 o'clock). This he avers is the only piece of evidence against his client (this is not true if William Jones' evidence is accepted), for if he had not gone to the stable that night then he would not have be standing in the dock.

Then he addresses the question of times in order to try and disprove opportunity. His argument is thus. Richard Williams went to Gaerwen after 6 o'clock, by one witness, Margaret Roberts, it was between 6 and 7. Owen Owen had then said that he remained there for well over two hours and a half (this is incorrect Owen Owen Senior states that he remained a little over two hours, where as his son Owen Owen Junior said over two hours not quite two hours and a half.) So if the witness, Lloyd went on, said that Richard Williams had not left Garnedd until after six then it must have been a considerable time after 6.30 when he arrived at Gaerwen (again this is contentious for even allowing for the tardiness of an old man he would have made the journey in less than15 minutes). If it was accepted that he stayed for two and a half hours then it must have been about 9.30 when he started home and it would have been 10 o'clock when he reached where the body was found. It does not take a mathematician realise that Lloyd it talking utter nonsense, and is reaching into the very bottom of the barrel.

In an attempt to strengthen this Harry Owen's testimony is referred to. Harry lived in Ty'n Rhos on the road between the Black Lion Inn and Llanddeusant. It was he who ran the Shoe Club that met at the chapel. Harry seems a stickler for accuracy, and it is he who addresses the time question.

'I called over the names of the members at seven the Garnedd boys were not present. I called at half past seven and they were present. Our time (chapel time) was about 10 minutes faster than 'railway time'. The 'country time' (local time) is from 20 minutes to half an hour than chapel time. I saw the Garnedd boys go home, I walked part of the way with them. I was home by 9.30. They had a shorter way to go than I did.' [19]

Questioned by Lloyd he said that they might have been home by 9.00 to 9.10 'railway time.'

It has been worth presenting this evidence in full if only to underline the confusion about time when a man's life could depend on minutes. But the point that he is trying to make is that Rowlands had been at Garnedd all the time the boys were there (Richard Roberts' testimony), or to put it another way Rowlands had not gone out until after they had gone to the shoe club, and had returned before they did. Lloyd argued that that he was therefore back even before Richard Williams had left Gaerwen. A more careful examination of the times will be made later to try and get order out of chaos.

Lloyd then dealt with something important, and something that could have been stressed more fully. He said that the evidence that was heard in court that day, important evidence, was given after the coroner had held his court, although it was known at the time. Even the judge mentioned that he had never heard such a difference in testimony between inquest and trial. When questioning William Jones, Lloyd had asked him why he had not mentioned the evidence that he had given in court that day to the coroner during the inquest, Jones replied that he had been scared and had been told just to answer the questions asked of him, but he spoke later '*to Mr Williams of Llanfairyn-*

[19] Harry Owen. *Trial CDH NWCH YHG*

ghornwy (Rev James Williams, J.P.) and to Mr Pritchard (Clerk to the Magistrates). Margaret and Richard Roberts also said that much of the evidence given at the trial they had first told to '*Mr Prichard after the inquest*'. It would appear that there had been a major enquiry immediately after the coroner's jury had brought in their verdict on the 7th November 1861.

Lloyd then remarks on the fact that the prisoner had not been questioned at the inquest nor been allowed to speak for himself (it will be remembered this could not by law have happened at the trial). The explanation that he had given to the police, he said, that he had been at the stable during the time he was out, he had never varied, and '*much of it was confirmed by witnesses for the prosecution*'. And as to the point about not going to seek the old man on the night in question, '*the jury had heard that he had stayed up until midnight*' (incorrect; Rowlands had gone to bed at 10 and it was Elinor and her son Richard who had stayed up until midnight), but if it was Rowlands that had murdered the old man would it not have made sense for him to make a show of searching for him. The reason that he did not go in search of his father in law was because was because the old man did not approve of people going out looking for him, and he had been out late often. In effect he is saying that this showed that Rowlands had no idea that the old man had been killed.

There was the evidence of Owen Owen Junior who stated (quite differently to what he said at the inquest) that he clearly heard Richard Williams calling out '*Richard*' from the direction of the boundary fence, although it was doubtful that he could have heard it from that distance (it is possible to discern sounds from someone hailing from the boundary fence, but it is not possible to recognise words clearly. It would have been even more difficult to hear on a thundery, stormy night, such as it was at the time, so Owen's inquest statement that he heard a 'cry' is easier to accept). Lloyd continued;

'Was this more likely a cry of remonstrance? Being near his own house where he knew his son-in-law and grandson were, was it not reasonable and natural that the unfortunate deceased attacked by some ruffian in the field called out for help to 'Richard' his son-in-law, or 'Richard' his grandson – which considered in that light was a demonstrative fact in favour of the prisoner. Further Owen Owen said he heard the voice (sic) of two persons and that he knew the voice of one but not of the other. Thus they were fortified in their supposition that the other voice was that of a stranger, and not the voice of Richard Rowlands who was well known to him from his infancy.'

Dealing with the matter of the 'blood on the whisker' Lloyd points out that if Rowlands had been guilty why had he not washed it off in some pool of water thus avoiding suspicion. However, even accepting the bloodstain as fact, the way it is reported makes it obvious that Rowlands knew nothing of it. Morgan Lloyd however does say that the blood was more likely to have been because Rowlands had been in contact with the body that morning before he came to beg the assistance of William Jones, this is actually a good point, but it was ignored. Of the waterlogged footmarks, Lloyd said that was always possible in a marshy place like that and at that time of year.

He appealed 'with confidence' to the jury for a verdict of 'not guilty'. Why, he asks, should Rowlands perpetrate the foul deed attributed to him?

'Was there a tattle (shred) of evidence to show why he should do it? Why should he imbrue his hands in the blood of his father-in-law? He could account for a man committing an enormous crime from a passion of jealousy of kindred feeling, but not to jump at once to the greatest crime without provocation.'

This introduces a ploy that had been used by the great Scottish advocate John Inglis in the trial of Madeline Smith for murder of her secret lover Pierre Emile L'Angelier under Scottish law some five years earlier. The offender, said Lloyd, echoing Inglis' words, will commit crimes step by step until they become hardened and able to do any iniquitous act. It is only then that they commit murder. It is entirely possible, of course, given his reputation, that Rowlands had committed those 'step by step' crimes that Lloyd refers to.

The evidence against Madeline Smith was more conclusive than that against Rowlands, but Inglis secured a verdict of 'not proven'. There are some differences of course; the 'not proven' verdict is not available to an English Court, Madeline Smith was an extremely attractive woman from a wealthy family, and Morgan Lloyd quite definitely was not John Inglis.

The defence then reminded them that it was the task of the jury to consider whether the man in the dock was the perpetrator of the crime, and if they had any suspicions to the contrary they had to give him the benefit of the doubt.

'At present,' he continues, 'there may be some obscurity over the case which in the course of time may be cleared up. It was a case of mere suspicion, circumstantial evidence. If they convicted him the consequences would be utterly irremediable.'

With this parting shot, Morgan Lloyd rests his case.

Chapter 12
The summing up by Sir Henry Keating

For the fourth time in the combined hearings of the inquest and the trial an official of the courts when addressing a jury warns them to dismiss anything they had heard about the case and that they should decide on the evidence alone and not upon any rumours which (they) may have heard out of doors.

Sir Henry acknowledged 'that the evidence was purely circumstantial which was often very strong in bringing a conviction home to the minds of the jury but they must be careful not to connect anything in evidence that did not have a natural and necessary connection' (in other words they were allowed to draw inferences as long as those inferences were based on solid evidence). 'If', he went on, 'after considering the evidence it did not satisfy them beyond a reasonable and fair doubt that the prisoner had committed the murder it was their duty to say that the prisoner was not guilty. It was not for the prisoner to prove his innocence. If however the evidence brings to their minds that he was the person who committed the crimes, then they ought not to be deterred by any consideration from saying so.'

And so the jury retired to consider its verdict and the life of a lower class individual who had no permanent employment, semi illiterate, and unable to understand a word of English was trusted to a jury of the county's most affluent inhabitants.

Chapter 13
'What did the witness Ellen Hughes say?'

Juries in those days must have considered themselves the most put upon of people. Called to sit in judgement on a fellow human being, they were forced to sit for hours listening to legal rhetoric in the most uncomfortable of circumstances, and then asked to consider their verdict but promised no refreshment until they had agreed upon that verdict. It is no surprise that deliberations were conducted speedily, and were usually finished in less than an hour. The old saying 'Men must hang so jurymen may dine' was probably quite true.

This particular jury was out for about fifty minutes, when the foreman returned and sought permission to ask a question. This was granted and he wanted to know whether the witness Ellen Hughes had said anything about the prisoner going out a second time on the fateful night. The judge read out the whole of Ellen Hughes statement to the jury, and they retired a second time.

After ten minutes they returned and brought in a verdict of '*Guilty*'.

When the judge asked if there was any reason why sentence of death should not be passed, this was translated for Rowlands who responded with '*di-euog*' – 'not guilty', whereupon the judge placed the black cap upon his head.

It was reported in the press that that Sir Henry intoned the verdict in an affecting way. Rowlands was led out of the court, only to be brought back because on being asked if he had understood the sentence, he replied in the negative. The verdict given in English by the judge had not been translated for the non-English speaking Rowlands. On hearing the translation, Rowlands threw himself down and wept. After cursing the police and the witnesses especially William Jones for making up the case against him, he was taken to Beaumaris Gaol to await execution.

CHAPTER 14
In Prison

Immediately following the trial we have very little information about the prisoner other than that he was eating normally.

Perhaps we should leave it to *The North Wales Chronicle* of the 29th March 1862 to give a hint of what was happening inside that sombre cell where the last few days of a man's life was being spent.

'This unhappy and now notorious person continues to maintain in gaol that dogged demeanour which he adopted during the course of his trial and which he only temporary departed from in the excitement following his sentence. We are informed that he is not unwilling to convene on the subject but he is not encouraged to do so. His sole spiritual advisor at present is the Reverend H Hughes, Calvinistic Minister, Beaumaris., who is in daily attendance upon the unfortunate man, and to who's administration we are told, he pays profound attention. He expresses great contrition for the dissolute life he has led (he admits to have led) and the great Mercy that God has vouchsafed to him. He persists however in denying his guilt of this particular crime and declared at one time. that he could not forgive the jury or the witnesses who had brought this dreadful sentence upon him, but yesterday (Friday) he communicated to the above minister that he fully forgave all as he expected to be forgiven by his heavenly father, Notwithstanding he repeated with strong emphasis that he was innocently convicted of the murder of his father in law.

It is for all Christian people to use their prayers that this frame of mind may leave him, for so long as it continues the ministrations of those who seek to prepare him for his impending death are of little use, although he has been told that he has not the faintest chance of a reprieve it is believed that he will trust to a faint hope.

We are sorry that many unfavourable stories are going about concerning him. All who hear them should remember that in all cases of condemnation to death similar reminiscences are invented. In a country where capital punishment is so rare the interest being redoubled only adds to the fertility of the gossip. Rowland has enough to answer for in the crime for which he is to die and all those who hear such talk would do better to pray for him than to circulate such reports.

We believe that he has expressed a desire to see his wife his mother and his eldest son who have been communicated with by the authorities.

The execution it is now known will will take place on Friday next at eight o'clock in the morning. The executioner engaged by the Sheriff is the noted Calcraft.

A memorial to the Secretary of state has been originated by some parties in Beaumaris, for a commutation of the sentence, and has already received several signatures on the ground that the evidence did not sufficiently justify the verdict, but we think that there will be little hope that the prayer of the petitioners will be answered.'

Then there came an account of his final days 'the most

striking feature of which was his unaccountable persistence in declaring his innocence under the 'most solemn and truth inspiring circumstances'. They had been favoured they said with most of the following diary through the kindness of the Reverend Hughes, Calvinistic Minister of Beaumaris who had visited the prisoner once a day since the trial.

But first we have details of a petition made on his behalf to Sir George Grey, the then Home Secretary, dated the 27th March 1862. The following is an English translation of the petition as it appeared in *Yr Herald Cymraeg.*

We, whose names appear below, namely Ministers of the Gospel and others from the town of Beaumaris and its neighbourhood, wish in the most respectful way to call your direct and most serious attention to the following points:

1.   That a man called Richard Rowlands has been found guilty in Beaumaris, Anglesey, on the 22nd March inst. of the wilful murder of one Richard Williams of Llanfaethlu of the same county.

2.   That we your humble petitioners, after hearing the trial, and after paying as much attention as to every piece of evidence brought forward, believe it to be in every respect extremely circumstantial, and in our opinion, far from being sufficiently conclusive to justify taking a man's life.

3.   That we firmly believe that the anxiety shown by the prisoner after rumours began circulating about him, and the words that passed between him and some of the witnesses, such as William Jones, Ellen Hughes and the two policemen is no more suspicious that which would naturally be felt and shown by any person so accused, even though that person be innocent, under those unfortunate circumstances.

4. That the Judges clear and concise summing up, when considered by any intelligent and unbiased person present at the trial, was favourable to the prisoner. So much so that when a verdict of guilty was returned he was completely unprepared to accept the statement.

5. That no motive was advanced by the prosecution for the crime.

6. That the Honourable Justice Keating, when passing sentence, did not as was usual, say that he agreed with the verdict, or that the jury had come to a fair verdict based on the evidence brought before them. This is taken by many to mean that the judge did not agree with the verdict.

7. That we, your humble petitioners, have taken the liberty of sending you in this post a copy of one our local newspapers which contains a fair report on the trial and we humbly draw your most urgent attention to it.

8. We humbly hope that you, after giving consideration to the points we have raised, will find sufficient reason to petition her Majesty to consider the prisoner in a more forgiving and merciful light.

It is interesting to note that William Jones was one of the signatories.

We pick up the story again on March 31st from the journal of the good minister, and as is to be expected it is coloured by vivid religions sentiments and rhetoric, but through it we can recover some of Richard Rowlands' last days on earth, and get an insight into the psychological trauma he went through. On this particular day Richard was calm and collected. His serious position was the subject of discussion with the Reverend Hughes. Rowlands wondered at the long suffering of the Almighty in allowing him to commit so many heinous sins as he had committed during his lifetime - he admitted to the crime of seduction, He was then encouraged to admit his last great sin (i.e. that of murder) but Richard turned and looked seriously at the Minister and said, 'My dear Mr Hughes, I would never refuse to tell you if I were guilty of such an act. But indeed I am perfectly clean of the blood of the old man. I can say that now there is but a short step between me and death.' More in keeping with Richard's character perhaps was his unwillingness to forgive William Jones of Brynteg. That man he said had told a great many lies about him, He had not, for instance, told him that there was blood on his whisker. The Reverend Hughes then delivered a short lesson on forgiveness. On his next visit Richard thought he could forgive William Jones. When he was visited on Tuesday 1st of April the conversation seemed mainly philosophical, with Richard stating that he had thought that justice would work its way and that he would be freed but to his great disappointment this had not happened. The clergyman replied that a great many unjust things happened in this world, and that God would judge fairly in the end. Richard Then thought that 'if he were liberated he would follow a different course of life, and this melancholy event would be a blessing.'

So Tuesday passed into Wednesday the 2nd of April.

The day saw two important events. The petition to Sir George Gray the Home Secretary had been answered. Rowlands had not been informed of this petition in case his 'hopes were falsely raised', but he was now told that it had been refused. He did not seem the least distressed, and when asked he said he had not expected his life to the spared.

The reply was worded thus:

'Sir,

Sir George Grey has given the case of Richard Rowlands, prisoner under sentence of death, his most urgent attention on behalf of those who appealed to him, and he has informed me to advise of his regrets as he can find no sufficient reason, in accordance with his official duty, to advise her Majesty to interfere with the course of the law.'

The response was over the hand of H Waddington.

The main event was a visit by members of his family. This happened about 2 o'clock in the afternoon. They were there at Richard's request. Present were Elinor his wife, his son of about 15 or 16 by his first marriage, Hugh Rowland, his brothers John, Thomas, and Hugh, and his nephews James and William Roberts. Three Ministers of the Gospel were also present, The Rev. Dafydd Griffiths, Chaplain of the Gaol, The Rev. Dr Henry Harris Davies[20], Curate of Beaumaris, and the Rev. Hugh Hughes Calvinistic minister of Beaumaris.

After a tearful welcome, the prisoner dropped to his knees and prayed for forgiveness Once again he said that he was, 'innocent as a new born child'. This, he said he declared before his family, three Ministers of the Gospel and "In the presence of God, before whom I shall be judged the day after tomorrow.' Again he referred to William Jones saying that he had told an untruth and that this was his greatest stumbling block in his way on the road to salvation, that he could not 'bring himself to forgive him!' He added that he had himself been very wicked and that he wished his son to

---

[20] It is interesting to note that Davies was convicted for poaching 5 partridges and was ordered to pay £5 fine or serve seven days in prison. He paid the fine, but one must ask why he committed the crime.

follow a different course of life. He handed a Bible to the Rev. Davies and asked him to read a portion of it as a blessing upon the counsels he had just given his family. Several such readings took place and several prayers were said. The two hours his family spent with him proved to be a harrowing experience. One brother was too overcome to say anything, his son had to be taken from the room, he was so distressed, and Elinor actually fainted.

It is after this visit, or perhaps after the refusal of clemency, which, although he may have been ignorant of the petition, it might still have sounded rather final to him, and would have extinguished any hope he had entertained of being pardoned or reprieved. It does appear that after this time he loses his fortitude. A visit from the Rev. Robert Thomas of Beaumaris, his first visit as it happened, then occurred, The Reverend found him anxious, sorrowful and penitent. He read the 39th Psalm, and the 15th Chapter of Luke to him, and then the parable of the Prodigal son, after which Richard shouted "Diolch, diolch, diolch" - thank you.

Thursday 3rd April dawned and found the Rev. Hughes unequal to the task of visiting Richard alone, so the Rev. Thomas Independent Minister accompanied him. Richard was obviously dwelling more on his fate, thanking God for "preserving his sanity so he could think of the interests of his soul." Again he declared his innocence. Later in the afternoon they visited him again and found him to be almost in a dying state. His whole body shook in spasms and only the whites of his eyes could be seen. After a while he held the Rev. Hughes' hand for some minutes, after which the two clergymen decided to leave and call back later in about two hours, when they were able talk to him. He told them that he intended to address the people from the scaffold telling them that he was innocent, but he was dissuaded. The

Reverend Thomas then called again later but he was told that Richard was in a low slate physically. He called again at seven that evening and found him weak and distressed, Richard was urged once again to confess, but he said that he had nothing to reveal, and after reading a hymn to him several times, the clergyman wished him farewell, to which Richard replied, 'Farewell my dear friend.' Later that evening a service was being held in the prison chapel, and just before it ended footsteps were heard passing the door, and the voice of the prisoner, loud and painful, declaring that he had said goodbye to all his friends and relations, and now he would say goodbye to the world. He was being taken away to the yard so he could see the world for the last time

During the Thursday afternoon communion was administered by the prison chaplain, which was the first and last that Richard had received and it was said that it afforded him much peace of mind. He refused any meal that night, and slept soundly until 12 o'clock. At 4 o'clock he was visited by the Rev. Davies and J Williams Esq. the Undersheriff. At half past five the Rev. Hughes joined them. Richard professed to have acted upon their instructions, but asserted yet again in a most impressive way, his innocence, and his last act there was to take their hands and exclaim "Remember my last words, I tell you I am innocent of the crime for which I have been condemned.'

The last two hours of his life, were spent in hymn singing and praying. We can thank the Rev. Henry Harris Davies and *Yr Herald Cymraeg* for the account of his final hours on earth. The singing and praying, according to them was done to take his mind off the matter and to prepare him for his "far journey" (siwrnai bell). The prisoner took up his pipe often to help lessen the pain in his mind.

"Dear Reader," said the Reverend Davies, "That hour was

a terrible hour indeed." The two other Clergymen present were trembling uncomfortably, and weeping 'like children" Richard asked what time it was and when told it had just struck 7 o'clock he remarked that time was passing slowly, and that his time was nearly at an end. He regretted that he had to say goodbye to all his friends and relations, but nothing compared to having to face eternity. Davies then told him that he could not hope for his soul's salvation if he still continued to maintain his innocence if was indeed guilty. He said, "The awful moment in too near for me to lie to you all. If I had anything to reveal I would do so now. He had said that he wished to declare his innocence on the scaffold but, said Davies, he was persuaded not to, and that the clergymen would make sure that everyone knew that he had not confessed to the crime. The Rev. Davies continues, "It in now a quarter to eight and I can hear the sound the crowd outside, and then I heard the church bell ringing." He confessed that he had begun to tremble, upon hearing the prison Chaplain reciting the solemn service for the dead outside the cell door, and that for a man who was still alive! Had he been able to flee the terrible place there and then he would have done so. Then the governor of the prison (Mr John Jones) came in followed by the two sheriffs, and then ''that unfeeling (perhaps unemotional) man Calcraft', the hangman. He pinioned the prisoner in a very short space of time, and Richard offered no resistance. The prisoner then shook hands with everybody (the prisoner prior to his or her execution was at this time pinioned with the arms in the front). He walked calmly to the scaffold, stood equally calmly as the noose was placed over his head. He shook hands with the executioner, and then the bolt was drawn. Death was believed to be instantaneous. It appeared to the Rev. Davies that he died a penitent man.

A reporter outside the gaol witnessed a huge crowd gathering, some having arrived the night before. He believed there must have been 5000 present although this is unlikely. As the sombre cortege appeared on the scaffold a low murmur began among the crowd, which grew louder by the second and rising to a shriek when the drop crashed down. Many amongst the crowd fainted at the dreadful sight. The reporter was surprised by the number of young ladies in the crowd, all dressed in their very best clothes. This appeared to be true of most public executions

Chapter 15
Letters to the press

An entry in the Register of Deaths for the 12th of May 1862 records the death of Richard Rowlands by judicial hanging in Beaumaris. The report was made by one Robert Roberts who it is stated was present at the death. This could possibly be some relation of Elinor by her first, late husband, or some official of the town, but this remains conjecture.

Interest in the case, which was set aflame by the inquest, was all but extinguished by news of the death of the Prince Consort in December 1861. But there was a ballad penned, in his inimitable way, by Abel Jones, 'Y Bardd Crwst', after the inquest which really only put the newspaper reports into verse, and nothing new is learned, apart from the fact that Abel Jones did not doubt Rowlands' guilt.

The trial and execution reignited the interest, and the press became the arena for the battle of words and opinion that vied for column space. What one comes to realise is that before the trial no-one seemed to doubt Rowlands' guilt, but after the passing of the death penalty opinion became immediately divided.

Almost immediately after the trial two more ballads were penned in the usual sensational style, which again merely told the story with the assumption that Rowlands was guilty, and as was usual with this kind of literature, there was a moral ending exhorting the youth of the day not to make the same mistake as Rowlands did. Ballads, obviously, were the bread and butter of the balladeer and they had to be readable and exciting for them to sell. The fact that there were two ballads written suggests that there was competition among them, so perhaps we should not cavil too much at them for a bit of sensationalism. (See appendix)

It is to the 'Letters' section of the papers that we should look for our next source of information. Letters seem to fall into two broad categories, although the usual melee occurs with one correspondent attacking another. Firstly, there were those who considered that the evidence was insufficient to warrant the death penalty and that transportation would have been a more suitable punishment. Secondly, there were letters concerning William Jones, either that he was a liar, (who had either given false evidence or had elaborated his evidence), or there were those that supported him.

Some of the letters that fall into the first category also bear testimony to the fact that even in the mid 19th Century there was a strong body of opinion against capital punishment, but over a hundred years would elapse before it would be abolished for murder and over one hundred and thirty years before it was struck off the statute books altogether.

But first let us quote 'The Welsh Girl'.

The Welsh Girl had a regular slot in *The North Wales Chronicle*, and although there appears to be little information about this correspondent, 'she' was probably a 'he', but for convenience sake it will be assumed that 'she' was indeed feminine. She hailed from Clynnog supposedly, and her column always dealt with some piece of contemporary news in a satirical manner, but hidden in the humour there was sometimes a nugget of gold. On the Rowlands affair she opined that being only a girl she couldn't possibly be expected to comprehend the ins and outs of the case, and she couldn't understand what all the fuss was about (the war of words in the papers) since the man (Rowlands):

'... in his anxiety to prevent people from thinking it was him almost told right plain that he did commit the murder. Why the man almost said himself that he did it.'

Since Rowlands had denied his guilt to the end, her words are obviously sarcastic, but maybe this was her way of drawing attention to this. Many others thought the same.

On Saturday the 29th March 1862, *Yr Herald Cymraeg* published its report on the trial of Richard Rowlands. He was now languishing in Beaumaris Gaol some six days away from his execution. The paper also contained a few verses penned by Iorwerth Llwydfryn entitled '*Llinellau Byrfyfyr*' (translated – Impromptu Lines). In them he expressed some sympathy with the plight of the condemned man, and wondered how a human being, wrought in the image of God, could be condemned to die on the 'cursed tree'.

He hopes that the unfortunate will beg the grace of God and thus secure for himself eternal life; he also feels pity on the mother who bore and nursed him. But it is the final verse that is most telling where he wished that he could release him and send him to languish in some foreign land under some sort of punishment until de died there of natural causes.

The five verses he wrote tells of one who is opposed to the death penalty, and also one can glean that perhaps transportation would have been a more fitting punishment.

The North Wales Chronicle of April 12 contained three verses by John D Davies, Llangefni entitled, 'Is capital punishment justifiable?' in which he proclaims his contempt of the hangman and his office.

Then we think the hangman's office
Ought not to endure
Cruel quarks are not our doctor
Killing is not our cure.

And 'tis portion of our compact
Sworn with earnest faith
That we make a sinecurist
Of this man of death.

Both his trade and his example
Out of date are gone
Aid the plot and pass the watchword
On forever on.

Thomas Jackson of Holyhead wrote in the same issue obviously inspired by Rowlands' execution:

Behold the culprit, trembling with fear,
Now reigns a solemn pause,
Through all the gazing crowd!
The pointed spears,
Glittering advance to the fatal spot –
The woe-worn victim
Lifts his trembling hands bedewed with sweat
Towards heaven his only refuge last resource
And seems to pray devoutly –
And yet while the faltering accents tremble on his lips
Behold the drop falls from beneath his feet
The pliant chord draws close and stops his breath.

Much of the correspondence, however, centres around William Jones, Brynteg, until it eventually descends into a slanging match between those who thought him a liar (mainly Pererin, the Rev. Henry Harris Davies who had attended Rowlands in the death cell) and those who supported him.

Ioan Gwynedd corresponding in the April 19th issue of *Yr Herald Cymraeg* referred to people who thought they had spotted something in a report of the trial. When William Jones gave his evidence at the trial he deposed:

'I recollect the prisoner coming to my house on the 2nd of November. I told him there was blood as I thought on his whisker. I saw it exactly like blood. He wiped the clean side of his face and I told him that is not the side, it is the other side. He turned after he wiped it and asked, is it clean now? I said no it is there still, and there I saw it, the last thing after I spoke to him. Then we went to the body.'

The implication here of course, is why William Jones would think the blood suspicious if he had not known of Richard Williams' death when Rowlands visited him. The blood might, after all, have been inflicted by a razor.

Ioan Gwynedd put the matter right. He was, he said, present at the trial. According to him what was actually said by Jones was that the prisoner came to him in the morning of the 2nd November and told him that the deceased had been found dead in a ditch, where he had fallen in, and he wanted Jones to come with him to help carry the body home. It was then that Jones mentioned that there was blood on his whisker.

And so the slanging match continues

Here is one correspondent whom we only know as Gwirionedd (Truth):

'I am sorry that Pererin and other preachers who consider themselves to be respectful see fit to talk so much in an underhanded way without considering that by so doing they border on slander when questioning the characters of the respectful jurors and witnesses at the trial. If these people knew what sort of man Richard Rowlands was during his lifetime, the heinous acts he had committed as a prelude to the gallows, they would never utter a word about the faithful and truthful William Jones.'

The *heinous acts*, not 'crimes' it must be noted, mentioned remain unknown, but it must be remembered that Rowlands was denied membership of the church in 1859. These heinous acts could well have been of a sexual nature, such as adultery, which, although it is not condoned, is not considered such an appalling act today.

William Jones also sent letters (certainly written on his behalf) to the press (*Yr Herald Cymraeg* originally), saying that he had only told the truth and that he had been happy to sign the petition to save Rowlands' life. He also forwarded a letter written to him by Pererin to the Herald. Pererin himself was not happy that Jones had done this as he believed that Jones and his supporter Gwirionedd were not worth being acknowledged in any newspaper.

The letter that Pererin had sent Jones is as follows:

'If you ever come to Beaumaris again, call on me, and I shall tell you some secrets that you would not want anyone to know, and I do not, naturally, for your sake, intend to tell them to a newspaper. Remember it is only you and I who know about them. If you are a man without blame yourself and if you have only told the truth, the whole truth as you shall answer for to God, then do not worry at all what anyone may say about you, but if the reverse is true than remember that all mysteries will be revealed on the Day of Judgement.'

There is a rumour, and that is all it is, that William Jones made a pass at Elinor, Rowlands' wife, There is no evidence of this at all but it is obvious that Pererin had got hold of something.

Cyfiawnder (Justice) was surprised that such a respectable man as Pererin should throw such unproven accusations both privately and publicly at William Jones, but on the 31st May 1862, one Williams of Beaumaris really took up arms, openly accusing Davies of using the affair for his own enhancement.

'There is an old saying (he writes) that 'the higher a monkey climbs the more he shows his tail'. And so it is with than man who calls himself Pererin of Beaumaris. He has shown the country by his stupid and insulting letter to one who is called William Jones of Brynteg that he is the keeper of a murderer's secrets (a low station for one who preaches the Gospel, don't you think?). We advise William Jones not to take any notice at all of anything that man writes. The whole of Dr Davies, PH, MA, Pererin's interference in the matter of the murderer Richard Rowlands is naked bombast, something akin to a mountain bearing upon a small mouse. When a street juggler comes to town one hears him beating loudly on an old drum that he owns in order to raise an audience. So does Davies beat his tiresome and tuneless drum for no other reason than to declare to the world that in Beaumaris, there is Pererin.'

The furore in the press had died down by the end of June and the whole matter passed into memory, but not before many people had begun to have second thoughts. What puzzled them most was the fact that if he was guilty why had he not confessed when he was under such immense pressure to do so, and although many were unwilling to state categorically that he was innocent, things seemed to imply that it was not impossible for it to be so. People had begun to appreciate that a life had been taken by the law on such sparse evidence.

Perhaps we should let Pererin have the last word on the subject after all. He said that there was a mystery pertaining to the death of Richard Williams that would, like all other mysteries, come to light on Judgment Day.

Chapter 16
Reflections

Anyone who has stayed the distance will probably know as much about the Richard Rowlands affair as is possible to know given the state of play at the moment. That is not to say that it is the end of the story for who knows what is hidden away in dark and dusty places waiting to be brought into the light of day?

Most people asked today if Richard Rowlands was innocent would probably say yes'. There are a number of reasons for this. Firstly and not least is the fact that popular opinion has him innocent, and that his conviction and subsequent execution was a miscarriage of justice. Secondly, there was no direct evidence for his guilt and precious little circumstantial evidence either, not enough to take a life, anyway. And there was that question of evidence rigging. What people mean is that they are given the evidence and are not comfortable with it.

In reality, of course, it is not that simple. At the trial of Rowlands the prosecution had to prove its case beyond the reasonable doubt. Today, to prove his innocence in retrospect, the case must be made for his innocence that is beyond a shadow of a doubt to be conclusive. Unfortunately as in most historical crimes, the evidence cannot be recovered. What would we not give for a glance at those original police documents, especially Richard Ellis' notebook. Unfortunately we must rely on press reports and these do not provide evidence.

There are some questions that must be asked.

Did the police have a case against Richard Rowlands? In other words did they put forward a valid motive for the crime; did they prove means and opportunity? And if they did, how well did they do on this occasion?

As far as motive is concerned, that given at the trial was the fact that Richard and his family were going to be evicted from the farm on the very same day that the murder occurred. That fact does not seem in dispute at all. Richard Williams was heard to say it sometime during the corn harvest of that year, and Elinor's first words to Rowlands on his return home on the fateful night was whether he had heard something about a house. What one must ask of course is, was this sufficient motive for murder?

Apparently, being evicted from one's home was very much a fact of life in those days, so for this to be considered a valid motive there must be more to it.

Here is a fairly young widow with four children and expecting another child. We can deduce that she was 7 months pregnant since it was said in evidence at the trial that she had delivered a full term child at the end of December. This would have been little Ann, Richard's daughter whom he never saw. Also at Garnedd was her father, Richard Williams. He was probably a typical, lower class, 'respectable' person to judge from what was said about him. Also putting in an appearance on what seemed to be a regular basis, at least weekly, was Elinor's new husband, Richard Rowlands, who was something of an unsavoury character. Such was the opinion of Williams of his new son-in-law that he had forbidden him access to the farm at first, only to relent later and allow him limited visiting rights. Friday seemed to be the permitted day.

There can be little doubt that his daughter's marriage to Richard worried him greatly. He did not attend their wedding at the Register Office (not a respectable church or chapel, note, although it could well have been as they had both lost their spouses) nor in fact did any 'family'. He would have been extremely sensitive to 'what the neighbours thought', especially as his daughter was carrying a child conceived out of wedlock. So all was not well between father and daughter. This fact is beyond doubt because Elinor when ordering a coffin for her dead father, insisted that it should be made of deal, not oak. It is known that deal was a 'poor' man's wood. It was deal she said that her father intended for the children, implying that he meant to leave them destitute, and without inheritance probably.

What all this suggests of course is that there was a great deal of tension inside the walls of the little farm.

It could also be that Richard Rowlands married Elinor with the intention of eventually becoming master of Garnedd, and in fact there is reason to believe that he may have even been grooming himself for that role. Although rejected, he did apply for membership of the Methodist Church in 1859. This was for some undisclosed misdemeanour, but the rejection rankled, and he said he should be judged for what he was now, not for what he had done in the past. Here perhaps is evidence of an attempt, albeit belated, to gain some respectability as befitted his vision for the future.

If we couple this with Richard's behaviour on the night of the 1st November, we can possibly disperse some of the shadows. He came home to learn that his father-in-law was still adamant that they should leave (his wife asking about a house). He asked where he had gone and after being told 'to Gaerwen' he went almost straight out after him.

So all that can be said with some degree of certainty is that the eviction from the farm was probably causing more concern to Richard and especially to Elinor than was initially appreciated. The motive could therefore be 'gain'. But the question must be repeated; was it a strong enough motive? All we can say is that it convinced the jury.

So what about opportunity? This is simpler.

Although he did not admit doing anything untoward, Richard did go out after his father-in-law, and return after the probable time that the old man was killed. He was not able to provide an alibi, and although this does not prove his guilt, it does not help his case. His remark to the police that he was 'pulling hay' for half an hour means nothing.

The whole question of time-keeping as mooted earlier adds layers of complication to the issue. It was rather clumsily, and rather half-heartedly used by Morgan Lloyd in the trial to try to establish that Richard could not have been present at the boundary fence at the time of the murder, but he was unconvincing.

The three time systems referred to earlier do complicate matters, but if one time system is adhered to a the following timeline does give Rowlands opportunity to be at the boundary fence at roughly the same time as his father-in-law, but only if we accept that he was absent for one and a half hours as given in evidence by Ellen Hughes at the trial. If the time of one hour that she gave at the inquest is correct then he could not have been at the boundary fence at the same time as his father-in-law. All times are in 'local time'.

6:00	Richard Williams leaves for Gaerwen
6:20	Richard Williams reaches Gaerwen at the latest
7:00	Richard Rowlands reaches Garnedd farmhouse
7:20	Richard Rowlands leaves the house
8:40	Richard Williams leaves Gaerwen
8:47	Richard Williams reaches the boundary fence
8:50	Richard Rowlands arrives back in Garnedd

If we consider the testimony of Harry Owen the organiser of the Shoe Club, matters are further complicated for he states that the boys returned home to Garnedd about 9;10 'railway time' which would translate to about 8:45 'local time', which only just makes it possible to place both perpetrator and victim at the crime scene at the same time; but only just.

Opportunity has been proved but has it been proved beyond a reasonable doubt? All we can say again is that it convinced the jury.

We move on to means.

'Means' is slightly more problematic. In a case of trauma any object lying around could be thought of as 'means'. Today, however, there would have to be something to link it to the crime. The head injury suffered by Richard Williams could be described as a concomitant, or 'eggshell' fracture, where the skull is depressed like an egg after being hit by a spoon. Without an ounce of justification Inspector Ellis claimed that a hammer found in the dairy was the murder weapon. We do not know what sort of hammer it was but we do know that an assault by such an object would leave an unmistakable indentation even with repeated blows. It could possibly be the hammer but no evidence given at either the trial or inquest proves this. Further more at the inquest/trial it was admitted by the police that no blood was found on the hammer. There are slight problems here also. On one of the few occasions when Richard's words are reported he is said to say to a policeman as he remained in custody at Holyhead Police Station after his arrest, 'Whatever killed the old man, that hammer never did'. That was taken as a mark against him i.e. that he knew what had killed the old man. But we cannot accept that 'means' was proved by any stretch of the imagination.

To sum up then - opportunity, motive, means; maybe, maybe, no. The police did not really have a case.

The second question must be; was he given a fair trial in the sense that the evidence was valid and that he was given the presumption of innocence?

Evidence was offered in the trial was mainly circumstantial apart really from the provable fact that he was out at about the time the murder was being committed.

Circumstantial evidence is tricky. One piece alone means nothing but many pieces together may 'point a finger'. Many things were only adduced at the trial alone. A fact that the judge and the defence commented upon.

Let it be made clear, however, that in the days before forensic science and DNA that the courts had to rely much on circumstantial evidence. Very rarely was a crime seen to be committed, and with no way of linking victim to perpetrator in a murder case, circumstantial evidence had to be accepted.

In Richard Rowlands case the points that were considered suspicious were the facts that his family was going be evicted, that he went out soon after asking the whereabouts of the old man, and returned just after the time the murder was supposed to take place; the fact that he expected everyone to lie for him to the police about his whereabouts on the night in question. Added to this it was considered suspicious that he did not wash his hands after he came to the farm the first time, but he did after he returned a second time. Also against him weighed the fact that he was in no hurry to get to work on the morning after the murder as he usually did (itinerant workers were probably employed on a first come first served basis). Finally the fact that Richard or his wife, Elinor, did not go out looking for the old man was considered suspicious indeed. Now as far as the Inquest was concerned that is all the evidence there was. Yet he was named in the verdict as the perpetrator.

Morgan Lloyd made a fair attempt in the trial to explain these things and indeed there is nothing in the prosecution's evidence that would justify taking a man's life. Perhaps the most telling thing he said was that if he had not been seen going out for a second time on the fateful night, he would not be in the dock fighting for his life. Without that piece of evidence the entire case against him falls apart. One can only wonder why Rowlands did not make some attempt to explain his absence that night.

The police were missing one vital thing, and that was something that would place him at the scene of the crime at the time of the murder. In other words a piece of incontrovertible direct evidence.

When the case came to trial on 22nd March 1862 the *Caernarvon and Denbigh Herald* excitedly reported that much new evidence would be adduced in court. One piece that differed was Owen Owen jnr report about the sounds heard to come from the boundary fence. At the inquest he heard 'a cry', at the trial this had evolved to the sound of two men quarrelling and the clearly enunciated name Richard. He confessed that he recognised the voice of the old man, but did not recognise the other. When asked how long he knew

Rowlands, he answered 'all my life'. The boundary fence is some 500 metres from Gaerwen and is not actually visible from there. One might conceivably hear a shout, but anything more is doubtful, keeping in mind that the night was thundery. However assuming that it was as reported at the trial it really amounts to nothing. There were a number of 'Richards' in the vicinity and since the exact time of death had not been established nothing was proved beyond the reasonable doubt.

Then came William Jones. At the inquest he had given his evidence in a quiet, subdued manner, but this was before Inspector Ellis informed the court that Richard Rowlands had told him that there was no enmity between the old man and anybody except William Jones. After this Jones' memory improved immensely because at the trial he had a lot more to say. Here now was the evidence that would put Richard Rowlands at the scene of the crime. Richard had come to seek Jones' assistance when the body was found. Blood upon his whisker; footprints, one under the body, obviously made after it started raining at 7 o'clock because they were filled with water; Richard's attempts to draw attention away from the crime scene and his insistence that the death was an accident; Richard imploring Jones not to tell anyone that the old man had been killed but to say it was accidental.

The fact that Richard had already visited the crime scene that morning with his wife should have caused some pause for thought and again Morgan Lloyd made an attempt to explain. As evidence it was practically worthless, and there can be little doubt that William Jones had been rehearsed at length between the inquest and the trial. Also one seems to sense Jones (who was considered a 'simple' man) having his two minutes of glory and basking in the attention.

Even Ellen Hughes, the so called American woman had

her own brand new nail to hammer into Richard's coffin, for she seemed more certain of her facts and stated that Richard had been out of the house for an hour and a half (an hour was stated at the inquest) stretching the opportunity element further. Her new confidence did not go unnoticed for the judge remarked that the witness' evidence was more 'favourable' than at the inquest. But Ellen Hughes had also said something else that was strangely admitted by the prosecution and ignored by Morgan Lloyd when he should have been ramming it down the throats of the jurors. Hughes had said that when Richard returned to the farm the second time there was no blood on him. A half-hearted attempt by Inspector Ellis at the inquest to suggest that there was blood on Richard's clothes was quashed by the coroner. So there were boundaries that even bias officials would not cross.

And to come in from a crime scene that by everyone's evidence was a bloodbath and have no blood at all on him ...?

It is regretted that modern forensic methods after such a time lapse remain largely silent. Inspector Richard Ellis made some crude attempt at gathering evidence when he cut some of the blood-stained turf from the crime scene, but no report is offered of any use he may have made of it. Some attempt can be made, however. It is known today that the blows to Richard Williams' head would not necessarily have killed him instantly and there is reason to believe that the blows were struck at the top of the boundary fence and that he fell or struggled down and thrashed round in the ditch. Behavioural analysis would tell us that 'overkill' i.e. repeated blows to a victim especially to the head is a rage killing, and often occurs when victim and perpetrator are known to each other. The only other thing worthy of note is the hole in the ground (or in the boundary fence, it is not quite clear in the reports) as if done by a pickaxe. It might suggest someone striking the floor in a temper and the handle of the pickaxe could easily have been the murder weapon. It was assigned some importance because it is mentioned by Ellis. We must, regrettably however, disregard this at the moment.

As to the presumption of innocence, it is known that tongues had begun to wag the morning after the murder to the extent that it worried Rowlands immensely and prompted him to seek the family's help in providing him with an alibi.

On more than one occasion the juries of the inquest and the trial were exhorted to forget everything they knew or may have heard about Rowlands and try the case on the evidence given in court alone. This is an extremely difficult thing to do, and present day jury members can be relieved if they admit to knowing the accused. Even today, the farming community is close knit, with everybody knowing everybody else. In the mid-Victorian era, lack of communications notwithstanding it must have been similar. Together with the reporting in the press at hysterical levels it is difficult to accept that the jury in Rowlands case knew nothing of him, and it is certainly possible that one or two of them may even have had a brush with him. At this time, however, this is only conjecture.

So almost certainly, given the weakness of the evidence adduced in court, his reputation almost certainly played a big part in getting him convicted. So we must regrettably say that he was not given the presumption of innocence which even today remains one of the cornerstones of British justice.

To move on to the verdict. The jury had some choice in the matter. They could find him not guilty, and so see him acquitted. They could find him guilty as charged, or they could find him guilty with a recommendation for clemency, which juries sometimes did if they found extenuating circumstances or points in the case that they found merited this.

This jury, however, we know, found him guilty as charged, with no plea for mercy. To find him innocent would have meant that the police had made a monumental mistake, and Rowlands would have left the dock a free man. If this is considered carefully the verdict was inevitable. We know that the deliberations went on for 50 minutes before a request was made to clarify a part of Ellen Hughes' evidence, namely the part that stated that Rowlands went out again that night and did not return for about one and a half hours, meaning he was in the vicinity of the crime when it was believed that it was being committed. Ten minutes later they returned with their verdict. This impresses people that the jury was giving the matter its careful and earnest attention, and suggests to those in the court that this particular piece of evidence was unclear to it prior to the trial. This, of course, was utter nonsense, for they would only have had to read the report on the inquest to learn this and it was widely reported. So it was a piece of theatre possibly staged to suggest, or more probably to emphasise, that it was this fact that had finally persuaded them, the only one piece of real evidence against him. Everything else could be explained away and indeed Morgan Lloyd tried to do this, but his efforts seem half-hearted, as if he knew he was already defeated.

It is extremely difficult to see how the jury reached their verdict unless one accepts that they considered Rowlands as someone who was entirely expendable. One is conscious of the fact also that it would have been highly unlikely that the case would have even come to court today, let alone end in a conviction. One cannot escape the notion that the jury had a hidden agenda.

Turning to the sentence. It has been noted that it was thought that the judge did not agree with the verdict. There is no evidence in the press reports that he openly expressed an opinion as the wording of the petition to Sir George Grey seems to suggest, but he certainly did not say that he agreed with the verdict, which judges tended to do. It must be remembered that once the verdict of guilty was brought in, the judge had no choice but to sentence the prisoner to death. It was not within his remit to do otherwise. Any decision for clemency would have to come from the Monarch via the Home Secretary. So in effect the sentence was unavoidable. The question to ask is this. Given all the anomalies, ambiguities and unfairness in the trial does one after all agree with the verdict? In other words despite all our misgivings do we consider the verdict safe? It is a difficult question. Perhaps even if the jury had access to a 'not proven' option the verdict would have been the same, but there are certainly those who would wish that Sir George Grey had been humane enough to commute the sentence to transportation. The petition on behalf of Rowlands for clemency strikes one as rather weak with no points being forcibly made, but rather just a copy of the report on the trial included. One wonders if the Home Secretary even read it. All in all, whether Rowlands was guilty or innocent, the verdict leaves a very bad taste in the mouth. And even given the more liberal acceptance of evidence in a court of law in the mid-19th Century one feels that a commutation of the sentence should have been ordered on the grounds that the evidence was so circumstantial.

Were there then any other suspects in the case? At the time, no. Ellis' investigations were scant to say the least. He had arrested Richard within two hours of arriving at the farm on what could only have been the fact that Richard was out at the time of the crime. No-one else came anywhere near the frame. Indeed if Richard Rowlands could have provided himself with an alibi, as he attempted to do so by asking Ellen Hughes to lie for him, the police would have had no viable suspect. But to darkness attaches myth.

There has emerged a story, unsubstantiated, that a prisoner in police custody in Caernarfon years later stated that he had killed an old man in the fields in Llanfaethlu. Although unproven this would explain a great deal. The near randomness of the crime and the fact that Owen Owen jnr did not recognise the second voice at the boundary fence. One says unsubstantiated, but Morgan Lloyd did make the point at the trial. The old man could have been attacked by a 'ruffian' in the fields, and called upon Richard his son in law or Richard hid grandson for help. Viewed in this light the evidence was in favour of the prisoner, he maintained. At the moment we must reluctantly discard this.

The other suspect dragged by myth into the frame is Elinor, Richard's wife. One certainly gets the impression that she knew more than is told. The furtive whispering in the bedroom on the morning after the murder; the reluctance to go to search for her father on the fateful night; and her obvious dislike, if not hatred of him as adduced by her wanting deal not oak for his coffin as it was deal he intended for the children. Couple this with the fact that even is she believed her husband's guilt it did not prevent her from visiting him in prison, nor fainting like a dutiful wife.

If one researches Elinor's story one finds a woman with 5 children one a babe in arms condemned to misery and to a social Siberia by the publicity of the trial and the judicial execution of her husband and father of her child. She reverts to her maiden name of Williams and goes to Llanberis, or at least to Caernarfonshire somewhere where she could have given birth by an unknown father to two girls. The 1871 census records two girls Jane and Maggie as being her daughters. When she returns to live in Llanddeusant (sometime before 1871) she is living as a pauper under her maiden name, and she retains this surname in 1881, although she has now become a 'housekeeper', and Jane and Maggie are her 'nieces'. By 1891 she seems to have acquired a house and is head of the family. She never remarried, she changed the name of the house to Garnedd the name of the farm she never inherited, and she reverted to the surname Rowlands, her husband's name. At least this shows a loyalty to her dead spouse. It doesn't prove that she killed her father but it does suggest either that she believed in Richard's innocence, or that she condoned his actions. Or did Richard Rowlands go to the gallows to protect his wife and new child never accusing, but always maintaining his innocence. It's an engaging thought until one remembers that Elinor was seven months pregnant. Would it have been possible for to have committed an act of murder out on a boundary fence in the dark.

CHAPTER 17
Final thoughts

The evidence does not prove Richard Rowlands guilt beyond the reasonable doubt, but neither can any solid evidence be found that definitely exonerates him, such as a cast iron alibi. In a Scottish court, as mentioned, such a case could have been 'not proven' (see the case of Madeline Smith who was judged so in 1858 even in the face of much more damning evidence). In a poll conducted on an internet site over 50% of those who responded (over 1000) considered the case against Rowlands not proven. And yet a jury of 12 men found him unanimously guilty. So what actually put his head in a noose on that fateful spring morning in 1862?

On the court evidence alone there can be little doubt that emphasis was placed on Richard's absence from the farm during the crucial hour or so on the night in question. This raises its head often during the story and it was about this piece that the jury asked for enlightenment during their deliberations.

Probably the reason for his conviction must be sought elsewhere. There can be little doubt that Richard's reputation played a large part in condemning him. The mid 19th Century was a time when social status, class and respectability meant everything. Those lower down in the social scale were expected to be 'respectable'. It even permeated the level of the extremely poor who were classified as either the 'deserving poor' or the 'undeserving poor'. The former could receive parish help in the form of a benefit payment, whereas the latter would be dispatched to the workhouse. Richard appeared to live very much on his wits. He was of above average intelligence, and he had taught himself to read Welsh, though not to write it. He did not have permanent employment but 'followed the threshing machine' as was often reported. There is also a legend about him in Llanfaethlu that he participated in bare fist boxing or fisticuffs, which was illegal, but profitable. He was also said to have spent most of his time in the Black Lion public house drinking. He was the very anthesis of what was considered respectable. Added to this is the inference that he might have abandoned his wife and children of his first marriage and had probably taken up with another woman possibly in Caernarfon. The chances are that he was promiscuous as he admitted while awaiting execution that his greatest sin was seduction. This would certainly have offended the sensibilities of the prudish, self-righteous Victorians.

Letters to the press following his conviction and execution testify darkly to his character. He contaminated all who came close to him said one correspondent. Another said that no-one would doubt his guilt if they knew what sort of person he was. He reached an apex of undesirability when he was refused membership of the church in 1859 for an unspecified transgression that the *Caernarvon and Denbigh Herald* opined would probably shock us if we knew what it was. Even at the trial the judge warned the jury that it was to forget everything they had heard about him and concentrate only on the evidence. Their question about his whereabouts during their deliberations was probably to give the impression that they were doing just this.

Whatever happened at the boundary fence between Gaerwen and Garnedd farms on that dark and stormy night in 1861 will probably forever remain a mystery, or as the Rev James Williams said at the time that only God would know the truth. But as stated at the beginning this book is less to do with proving Richard's innocence or guilt, but rather to present the known facts and to try to make sense of the case against him.

To conclude therefore. Here we have a man who is the complete opposite of what society at the time would have called 'respectable'. An itinerant worker, a frequenter of taverns, a dabbler in minor illegal activities, one who had abandoned his wife and children of his first marriage. But what would have counted heavily against him was his promiscuity, and his possible liaisons with married women. He had produced a child out of wedlock with Elinor, although he had later married her, and this was a cardinal sin. He would not have been popular.

When the murder was done and it was found that he had not only left Garnedd that night, but had left there with the hint in the air that he might be going after the old man. When he returned soon after the time the crime was supposed to have taken place, and acted in what was considered a suspicious manner, he was an obvious suspect. A fledgling police force, which was unpopular, would have to score a success, and if Richard Rowlands had not committed the crime, then they were going to be hard pressed to find another suspect. And of course, the ethos at the age was that it was better for 100 innocent people to die than for a guilty one to go free. The people who knew Richard and had to put up with him, and there can be little doubt that must have tried their patience, here was an opportunity to be rid of him. Richard Rowlands had probably made too much of a problem of himself and the opportunity arose to solve the problem.

It is significant that, as far as reports can be interpreted, no-one doubted his guilt before the trial and especially before his execution. It is only in their aftermath that questions were asked. When the gallows had been erected outside Beaumaris Gaol, it became the centre of morbid fascination. People, a report said, looked upon it with horror, until they remembered that it was for Richard Rowlands who had 'imbrued his hands in the blood of an old man'. This summarises people's attitude towards him before the execution.

After the execution the more discerning people and those with a social conscience were worried. It was not Richard's guilt or innocence that worried them but that he had suffered the extreme penalty of the law when the case against him was so weak. Even the judge had not said that he agreed with the verdict, which judges usually did in such cases, probably to reassure the jury. Many deemed transportation to have been a more suitable punishment, for as Morgan Lloyd said in his closing arguments, one if his more sensible statements, that capital punishment was irreversible, it could not be undone, if new evidence came to light in the future. It is surely this that worries us the most, just as it worried some people at the time, that he was convicted for a capital crime and paid the ultimate price on so little evidence, and most of it circumstantial.

Rowlands denied his guilt to the end, never wavering, but neither offering a word in his own defence. So vehement and convincing was he that the ministers of the Gospel who attended him during his final hours became convinced that he was innocent. And indeed, it does make one stop and think that in an age where the fear of God was in most people that he would not have finally confessed for the sake of his soul. This refusal to admit guilt influenced a large number of people when it became known to them after the trial. But was Rowlands bluffing? Knowing that if he did admit the crime then there would be no hope for him at all, and he would be always considered a murderer. Perhaps we should attach more to a little-known piece of evidence. When awaiting execution, and constantly being urged to confess, he said to his attendant minister, 'But I thought that you said that it was only to God that one must confess?' The reader must make what he or she wishes of that statement.

If Rowlands did not commit the crime then it would be extremely difficult to pin it on anyone, but that is a weak argument. For what it's worth as to Rowlands' guilt or innocence, as far as the author is concerned, the jury is still out, but the 'stranger in the fields' theory has much to commend it. The impression gained is that even if Rowlands was innocent, he probably knew something about the matter and could even have been shielding someone, if not his wife, as mentioned, then someone else.

So at the present state of play any opinion about his guilt or innocence can only be based on conjecture and worse still, guesswork. There is no doubt that the case will never be solved until Rowlands' whereabouts during that crucial hour or so that he was out of the house on the night of November 1st 1861. Perhaps something will emerge in the future that positively exonerates him or confirms his guilt, but until that happens then Richard's reputation and his story remain like his body on that fateful April morning when the gallows trap had sprung, suspended 'between heaven and earth'.

Appendix

CÂN ALARUS
YN RHODDI CYFLAWN HANES LLOFRUDDIAETH
RICHARD WILLIAMS,
Ffermwr yn y Garnedd
GERLLAW LLANFAETHLU SIR FÔN
Yr hyn a gyflawnwyd nos Wener, 1af o Dachwedd, 1861

Cymerwyd un Richard Rowlands i fyny, ac y dybiaeth mae
ef a gyflawnodd y weithred ysgeler hon, a chymerwyd i
garchar Beaumaris, Sir Fôn, i aros y Brawdlys nesaf.

Trigolion Gwynedd, mewn amynedd,
Da chwi'n llariaidd, dowch yn llu,
Gwrandêwch ar weithred, drist echryslon,
Hylla foddion oll a fu;
Trwy Llanfaethlu nine galaru,
Gofid syn yw traethu'r tro,
Pawb sydd yno yn wael, a wylant
Tra hyn a gadwant yn eu cô.

Ar nos Wener, cynta' o Dachwedd,
Gerllaw i'r Garnedd, bu'r hyll nôd,
Un Richard Williams, ga'dd farwolaeth,
Mewn llofruddiaeth hylla 'rioed;
Yr oedd yn ffermwr bychan diwyd,
Ac yn cyd-fyw a'i ferch ei hun,
Nes cwrdd a llofrydd anrhugarog,
Hyll afrywiog, llidiog ddyn.

Am saith o'r gloch, o'i dy 'madawodd,
I'r ffermdy o'r enw 'Gaerwen' sy'
Ac ni ddychmygodd gwrdd â gelyn,
A wnaeth y weithred oeraidd fu;
Ei ddiben yno oedd cael peiriant,
I ddod ato i ddyrnu ei yd,
Am naw gadawodd deulu'r Gaerwen,
I gwrdd a'r llofrydd fwria'i lid.

Yr oedd ei bibell yn ei enau,
Pan adawodd deulu'r ty;
Ni chyrhaeddodd ond hyd clawdd terfyn,
Cyn iddo gwrdd â'i elyn du,
Y farn gyffredin mae vyda morthwyl,
Y ddarfu'r diaflyn wneud ei waith,
Sef dwyn bwydhen wr ddiwyd,
Oedd yn hyfryd wrth ei daith.

Richard Roberts, bachgen ieuange,
A ga'dd ei yrru gan ei fam,
I edrych am ei daid i'r Gaerwen,
Ond gwelodd ef cyn dod i'r fan,
Yn y ffos yr oedd yn gorwedd,
Yno'n waelaedd yn ei waed;
A'r bachgen wnaeth y peth yn hysbys,
Ac at y fan yn union aed.

Ei gorff a gyrchwyd tua chartref,
Yr oedd yn gelain, dyma'r gwir,
Yr oedd ei ben ef wedi ei friwio,
O glust i glust caledi clir;

Yr oedd ei fenydd wedi eu fostio,
Trwm yw ceisio cofio's cur,
Dioddefodd gael ei ladd yn gelain,
Trwy waith aflawen satan sur.

Yr oedd pedwar briw echryslon,
Hyll archollion dyfnion dwys,
'Roedd un o'r rhai'n o hyd dwy fodfedd,
Ar ei ben er poena pwys;
Ar ben, y clawdd ei waed ganfyddwyd,
Ac am llatheni hyd y llawr,
Pa ddyn cynddeiriog, anrhugarog,
A fu mor lidiog lofrydd mawr.

A dau Feddyg doeth a'i chwiliodd,
Ac at ei golon r'aethant hwy;
A buan gwelsant ei fod tu fewnol,
Yn gryf ac iach heb unryw glwy;
Dydd Llun, y Cwest dechreuodd,
A dydd Iau y saithfed dydd,
Bu'ont am ddeuddydd hir yn parau,
A phawb oedd yno a'n bronau'n brudd.

A barn llofruddiaethdrom wirfoddol,
Yn erbyn Rowlands yno wnaed,
Ac fe'i ddanfonwyd ef i'r carchar,
Nes cael ei brofi am y brâd;
Pan ddel y Sessiwn fawr i'w farnu,
'Boed ein gweddi oll ag un,
Bod Iesu o blaid cyfiawnder goleu,
Sy' wedi dioddef i gadw dyn.

Rhyfedd, rhyfedd fel mae satan,
Yn cael gafael arnom ni,
Yng nghanol breintiau mawr Efengyl,
Hyn sydd ryfedd iawn i mi,
Fod y fath weithred mewn gweithrediad,
Yng nghyraedd yr Efengyl wiw;
Er maint o ddarllen a phregethu,
Ac hefyd ddwys weddio Dduw.

Sôn am waedlyd lofruddiaethau,
O dyddi dydd sydd yma a thraw;
Ar y dydd cyntaf o fis Tachwedd,
Rho'wd ynys Môn mewn poen a braw,
Y flwyddyn deunaw cant â thrugain,
A blwydd yn chwaneg gyda hyn,
A bydd son am oesoedd ddelo,
Am we y Garnedd ro'wd yn y Glyn,

Os euog ydi Richard Rowlands,
Teilwng iddo ddiodde' yn ddwys,
Gobeithio dengys Awdur Bywyd,
Pwy fu'n cyflawni'r penyd pwys,
Rho i ninau nerth i wylio,
Bob dyn yn effro dan y nén,
Rhag of i rwydau'r llew rhuadwy,
Ein denu mwy, Amen, Amen.

ABEL JONES, Bardd Crwst.

CÂN NEWYDD
YN GOSOD ALLAN
DDIENYDDIAD
RICHARD ROWLANDS
O BLWYF LANFAETHLU, MÔN
AM LOFRUDDIO EI DAD-YNG-NGHYFRAITH
SEF
RICHARD WILLIAMS
Ar Nos Wener, y 1af o Dachwedd, 1862

Ar y Don Fechan

De'wch, drigolion Môn ac Arfon,
Fflint, Trefaldwyn, Dinbych, Meirion,
Trigolion y Deheubarth hefyd,
I wrando ar hanes tra ddychrynllyd.

O fewn i Fôn, ym mhlwyf Llanfaethli,
Gwnai Richard Williams gyfaneddu,
Ei ferch a'i phlant oedd yno'r unwedd
Gydag ef yn ffarmdy'r Garnedd.

Ei ferch a ddarfu ail briodi,
A'i gwr wnai ganlyn peiriant dyrnu,
Richard Rowlands oedd ei enw,
Ar grogbren ddaeth i ddiwedd chwerw.

Nos Wener, sef y cynta' o Dachwedd,
Aeth Richard Williams mewn gwirionedd
I dy cymydog, sef y Garwen,
Lle bu yn eistedd oriau llawen.

Cychwyn adref mhen rhyw amser,
Ar hyd y llwybr, fel gwnai arfer,
Nes iddo gwrdd â'i greulon gelyn
'R hwn wnaeth ei ladd wrth glawdd y terfyn.

Fe glywodd rhai ei lais yn gwaeddi,
O! Richard! Pan yn ei galedi;
Ond nid oedd neb i'w gynorthwyo.-
Pryd hyn yr oedd yn gyfyng arno.

Fe farna rhai mai gyda morthwyl
Y gwnai gyflawni'r erchyll orchwyl,
Gan fod ei ben yn friwiau dyfnion
Drwy law'r filain â'i ergydion.

I'r ty yr aeth y mab-yng-nghyfraeth,
Ar ôl cyflawni'r hyll lofruddiaeth,
Gan olchi ei ddwylaw wedi'r weithred,
Rhag byddai dim o'r gwaed i'w weled.

Aent i'w gwelau'r noswaith honno,-
A Richard Rowlands wnai dymuno,
Am beidio d'weyd ei fod ef allan,
A'r rheswm p'am a wyddai'i hunan.

Yr wyr a'i i chwilio'i daid y borau,
Fe'i cai yn farw dan ei friwiau,
Rai dyfnion erchyll, wedi gwaedu,
Ar hyd y lle am rai llatheni.

Yno daeth y mab-yng-nghyfraith,
Ac amryw eraill o'r gym'dogaeth;

Ol ei draed oedd yno i'w weled,
Yn y fan lle gwnaed y weithred.

Gwnaed ymchwiliad gan feddygon,
Ac ar ei ben caed briwiau dyfnion;
R'r rhain â'u golwg yn ddychrynllyd,
Yr hyn fu'n achos dwyn ei fywyd.

Cwest y crowner a gynaliwyd,-
A Richard Rowlands a gymerwyd,
Am lofruddiaeth oedd wirfoddol,
Yn ôl eu barn yn gydwybodol.

I dref Beaumaris fe'i cymerwyd,
Ac yn y carchar caeth ei rhoddwyd,
I aros yno dan y cloion,
Hyd ddydd ei brawf, rhwng muriau mawrion.

Pan ddaeth y sessiwn, gael ei farnu
Yn awr ger bron y *Judge* a'r *juri*,
Gwadu wnaeth nad oedd yn euog
O'r llofruddiaeth annrhugarog.

'Nol cael pob tystiolaeth allan
Fe'i gaed yn euog o'r gyflafan;
Tyst ,nol tyst oedd megys cadwyn
Yn troi'n hollol yn ei erbyn.

Y Barnwr wnai gyhoeddi'r ddedryd,
Mai dyd oedd ef i golli wi fywyd,
Am iddo ddwys i weddio ar Iesu,
Fod ei ddyddiau bron i fyny.

Fe'i gymerwyd dan ei alar
Yn ei ôl drachefn i'r carchar;
Lle gwnai pregethwr ac offeiriaid
Weddio'n ddwys ar ran ei enaid.

Ar y pedwerydd dydd o Ebrill,
Rhyw luoedd mawr wnai ymgynull,
Tua'r derf o bob cyfeiriad,
I gae gweld ei ddienyddiad.

At y grogbren fe'i cymerwyd,
A'r cortyn am ei wddf a roddwyd;
A cha'dd ddyodden pump-a-deugain
Am ladd hen wr oedd pump a thrugain.

Trwy'r dorff y rhedai och ddychrynllud
Pan gwthwyd ef i'r tragwyddolfyd,
Ac yna'i enaid a ehedodd,
Lle mynai Duw yr hwn a'i rhoddodd.

Bydded i'w berth'nasau hawddgar,
A'i gyfeillion sydd mewn galar,
Droi mewn pryd at Iesu grasol
Cyn wynebu'r byd trag'wyddol.

Gweddiwn ninau'n ddyfal beunydd
Am dduwioldeb yn ein crefydd,
Cel y'n caer ar ôl y bywyd
O rifedi plant yn gwynfyd.